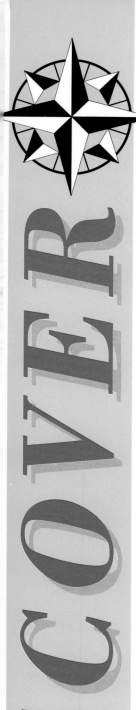

Human geography

Keith Grimwade

Head of Geography at
Hinchingbrooke School, Huntingdon

Hodder & Stoughton

A MEMBER OF THE HODDER HEADLINE GROUP

To the Teacher

This text is based on the First Edition of Discover Human Geography but it has been completely re-written. It meets the requirements of the new GCSE syllabuses.

Opportunities for developing essential skills have been included, and the way the text is structured makes it easy to select material to support schemes of work. Greater emphasis has been given to the study of specific places. The Enquiries help pupils to record important information and to develop their understanding of the themes covered; ideas for further research and for fieldwork projects are also included. Each section contains an assessment task which allows achievement to be demonstrated at a range of levels.

The style and format of the First Edition has been retained. The aim of the text also remains the same: to provide a thematic approach to GCSE Geography; to explore people-environment relationships; and to present information in an attractive, accessible and varied way.

A catalogue record for this title is available from the British Library

ISBN 0 340 593431
First published 1994
Impression number 10 9 8 7 6 5 4 3
Year   1998 1997 1996

This impression revised and updated 1995

Typeset by Litho Link Ltd, Welshpool, Powys.
Printed in Hong Kong for Hodder & Stoughton Educational, a division of Hodder Headline Plc, 338 Euston Road, London NW1 3BH by Colorcraft Ltd.

To the Pupil

This book covers the themes you need to study for the human parts of your GCSE syllabus. However, it is important to understand that human and physical geography are closely related: our "human home" is the "physical earth".

The Enquiries will help you to record important information and to develop your understanding of the themes covered. Ideas for your own fieldwork projects are also included. Please be safe: always work with a partner.

There is a glossary at the end of the book for you to use if you come across a word or phrase with which you are unfamiliar. Glossary terms are in **bold** in the main text. Use the index as well to find out where topics are mentioned.

Many geographical facts and statistics quickly become out of date. However, there is a wealth of information on the television and radio, and in newspapers and magazines: make use of these to keep up with current trends.

I hope that this book, together with its companion volume, *Discover Physical and Environmental Geography*, will make the world more interesting and more alive, and that you will want to visit many of the places written about for yourself.

Discover Geography!

ACKNOWLEDGEMENTS

The author and publishers thank the following for permission to reproduce photographs, diagrams and statistical information in this book:

J Allan Cash Ltd, Figs 184i&ii, 188; Architectural Association, Fig 43iii; The Geographical Association, Figs 24 & 29; Frieder Blickle, Fig 27; Angie and Rob Bruce; Jason Harvey, Fig 275; Hulton-Deutsch Picture Library, Fig 102; Mary Evans Picture Library, Fig 278; McGraw Hill Book Company, Fig 237; Office of Population Censuses and Surveys, Fig 7; Ordnance Survey for extract from 1:50 000 Ramsey map © Crown Copyright; Oxfam Project Partners, Fig 269; The New Internationalist, Figs 289, 295 & 296; Panos Pictures, Figs 79 & 128; Joanne Osborn, Fig 89; Philip Allan Publishers, Fig 32; Proton Cars, Fig 297; Robert Harding Picture Library, Figs 2v, 4iii&v, 34, 38, 77, 78, 80, 104, 119, 169, 193, 224, 265, 271, 280, 284, p.4, p.30, p.118; Routledge for extract from *The Third World City*, David Drakakis-Smith; Sylvia Cordaiy, cover photo, p.88, p.144, p.168; The Telegraph plc, Fig 106; Topham Picture Source Figs 33, 39, 82, 170, 182, 186, 268, 270; Traidcraft Exchange, Fig 298; Tropix Photographic Library, Fig 4iv.

All other photographs supplied by the author.

Every effort has been made to trace and acknowledge correctly all copyright holders but if any have been overlooked the publishers will be pleased to make the necessary arrangements at the first opportunity.

CONTENTS

POPULATION

1.1 *Where do we live?*

Population density

Population density means the number of people in an area. It is worked out using a simple formula:

$$\text{population density} = \frac{\text{number of people}}{\text{area}}$$

For example, you could work out the population density of your classroom. First, count the number of people in the room. Second, measure its length and breadth in metres and multiply the two values together in order to find its area. Then, divide the number of people by the area for an answer in people per square metres.

Population distribution

Population distribution means where people live. Some places have more people living in them than others (Fig 1) and a number of reasons help to explain this:

- **Relief.** This means the shape and height of the land. Steep, mountainous regions usually have low population densities because the climate tends to be harsh; there is very little flat land for farming and settlement and transport is difficult. Lowland regions are more likely to have high population densities because the climate is usually less extreme and farming, settlement and transport are easier.
- **Climate.** Although people can live in hot, cold and dry places – for example, the Innuit in North America and the Bedouin nomads in the Arabian desert – these regions can only support low population densities because there is not enough food and/or water. On the other hand, high population densities have developed where it is warm enough and wet enough for two or three crops to be grown a year.
- **Rivers.** High population densities are found alongside many of the world's great rivers because they provide water for drinking and irrigation, and they are a means of transport.
- **Type of farming.** Some types of farming can support more people than others; for example, shifting cultivation can support far fewer people than intensive rice cultivation (see Section 4.1).

- **Raw materials.** Mining needs relatively few people but raw materials can lead to the development of manufacturing industry (see below).
- **Manufacturing industry.** This leads to high population densities because factories need a large supply of labour. The growth of manufacturing industry has been a major factor in the development of towns and cities (see Section 2.8).
- **Transport.** Good transport links usually lead to high population densities because they make it easier for people to assemble raw materials, or to recruit workers, or to trade.

Fig 1   Why don't we spread out a bit?

POPULATION

Population distribution in the UK

In 1991 the UK's population was 57.8 million and its population density was 236 people per square kilometre. Its population distribution is shown in Fig 2.

Fig 2   Population distribution: the British Isles

(i) Population density

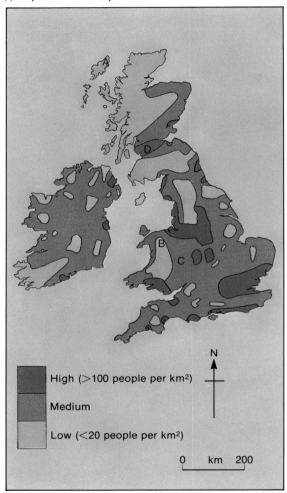

High (>100 people per km²)

Medium

Low (<20 people per km²)

N

0   km   200

(ii) Area A

(iii) Area B

(iv) Area C

(v) Area D

ENQUIRY

1   Use the map and photographs in Fig 2, and **thematic maps** of the UK in your atlas to help you complete a copy of Fig 3.
2   Use this information to help you describe and explain the distribution of population in the UK.

	A	**B**	**C**	**D**
Relief				
Climate				
Rivers				
Type of farming				
Raw materials				
Manufacturing industry				
Transport				

Fig 3 Population distribution: summary table

Population distribution in India

India's population in 1992 was estimated to be 883 million and its population density was 269 people per square kilometre. However, as in the UK, some parts of the country have very much higher population densities than others (Fig 4).

(i) Population density

1 Bombay
2 Delhi
3 Calcutta
4 Madras

high density
medium density
low density

(iii) Area B

(ii) Area A

(iv) Area C

(v) Area D

Fig 4 Population distribution: India

1   Use the map and photographs in Fig 4 (page 7) and thematic maps of India in your atlas to help you complete a copy of Fig 3.
2   Use this information to help you describe and explain the distribution of population in India.
3   Which factors seem more important in India than in the UK, and which seem less important? Suggest reasons for these differences.

1   Label on an outline map of the world these four major high density areas: North East America; Europe; South Asia; and East Asia.
2   Also label four major low density areas: the Arctic; the Great Deserts (label just one); the High Mountain Ranges (label just one); the Equatorial Forests (label just one).
3   Look at the photographs in Fig 6. Match these with the areas listed above and add their captions to your world map.
4   Which factors help to explain the areas of high population density?
5   Which factors help to explain the areas of low population density?
6   Why is the River Nile associated with a thin ribbon of high population density?
7   Compare Fig 5 with Figs 2 and 4 (pages 6 and 7). What do you notice about the amount of detail as the scale of the maps changes? Which factors are more important at the national scale and which are more important at the world scale?

World population distribution

Some of the factors which help to explain the population distribution of a country are also important at a world scale. However, other factors become even more important and the following Enquiry will help you to discover what these are.

Fig 5   World population distribution

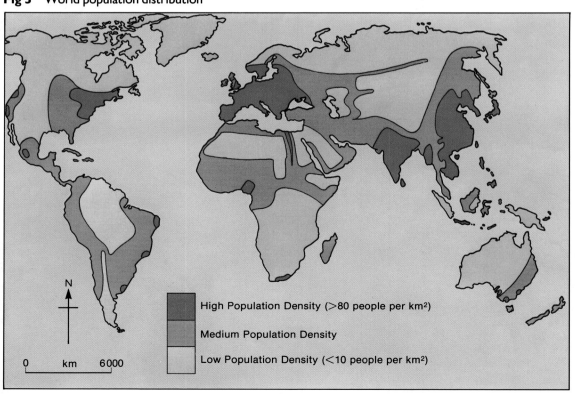

High Population Density (>80 people per km²)

Medium Population Density

Low Population Density (<10 people per km²)

0   km   6000

Fig 6 Population factors

(i) Equatorial rain forest

(ii) Raw materials

(iv) Modern farming

(iii) Manufacturing industry

(v) Dry climate

(vi) High crop yields

(vii) Steep relief

(viii) Cold climate

1.2 How many of us are there?

"How many of us are there?" is a difficult question to answer accurately. The United Nations estimate of world population – 5420 million in 1992 – is based mainly on census information and partly on special surveys.

A **census** is a 'counting' of population. It is not a new idea – for example, the Christian Bible tells us that Jesus was born in Bethlehem at the time of a census being carried out by the Roman Emperor. In Britain a census has been taken every ten years since 1801. Since 1945 most countries have carried out regular censuses.

You can see from the extract from the UK's 1991 census (Fig 7) that it does more than just count the number of people. Most censuses ask a range of questions and they provide a great deal of useful information. However, we must remember that the information might be inaccurate – for example, someone might give a wrong answer, and every day there are births and deaths.

ENQUIRY

1 Why do governments need to carry out censuses?
2 The UK census always causes problems. Why do you think some people dislike giving information about themselves on a census form?
3 Here is a list of information that could be asked for in a census – address, age, sex, marital status, citizenship, place of birth, occupation, income, religion, skin colour, disabilities. Which of these pieces of information do you think would be controversial and why? Compare your list with a friend's – do you agree or disagree with each other?
4 Why do you think it would be more difficult to carry out a census in a country like India than in a country like the UK?

1-3	**Name, sex and date of birth of people to be included**	**Person No. 1**	**Person No. 2**

Important: please read the notes before answering the questions.
In answering the rest of the questions please include:

► every person who spends census night (21-22 April) in this household, **including anyone staying temporarily.**

► any other people who are usually members of the household but on census night are absent on holiday, at school or college, or for any other reason, even if they are being included on another census form elsewhere.

► anyone who arrives here on Monday 22nd April who was in Great Britain on the Sunday and who has not been included as present on another census form.

► any newly born baby born before the 22nd April, even if still in hospital. If not yet given a name, write BABY and the surname.

Write the names in BLOCK CAPITALS starting with the head or a joint head of household.

Person No. 1

Name and surname

| Sex | Male ☐ 1 |
| | Female ☐ 2 |

Date of birth
Day   Month   Year

Person No. 2

Name and surname

| Sex | Male ☐ 1 |
| | Female ☐ 2 |

Date of birth
Day   Month   Year

4   Marital status

On the 21st April what is the person's marital status?
If separated but not divorced, please tick 'Married (first marriage)' or 'Re-married' as appropriate.
Please tick one box.

	Person No. 1	Person No. 2
Single (never married)	☐ 1	☐ 1
Married (first marriage)	☐ 2	☐ 2
Re-married	☐ 3	☐ 3
Divorced (decree absolute)	☐ 4	☐ 4
Widowed	☐ 5	☐ 5

5   Relationship in household

Please tick the box which indicates the relationship of each person to the person in the first column.
A step child or adopted child should be included as the son or daughter of the step or adoptive parent.

Relationship to Person No.1

Husband or wife	☐ 1
Living together as a couple	☐ 2
Son or daughter	☐ 3
Other relative	☐

Fig 7   Extract from the 1991 census

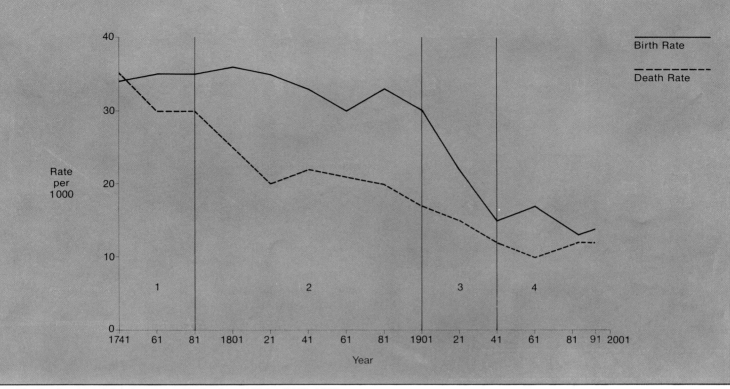

Fig 8 Birth and death rates in England and Wales 1741-1991

Population change in England and Wales

The population of some parts of the world is going up at a faster rate than it is in others. England and Wales is an area where there is a low rate of population increase at the moment and Fig 8 enables us to look at the balance between **birth and death rates** since 1741.

Fig 10 A British family today

Fig 9 A Victorian family

1   Make a copy of Fig 8 (page 11).
2   The graph is divided into four stages. For each of these stages choose the correct label from the following list:
— high birth rate and falling death rate
— low birth rate and low death rate
— falling birth rate and falling death rate
— high birth rate and high death rate
3   If stage two had continued what would have happened to the population of England and Wales?

The change from high birth and death rates to low birth and death rates in Fig 8 is known as the **demographic transition**.

In stage one death rates were high because many people were poorly fed and lived in unhealthy conditions. Also, even if people could afford to visit a doctor, medical knowledge was very basic. The population would have fallen if it had not been a high birth rate.

In stage two death rates began falling. At first this was probably because the agricultural revolution of the eighteenth century had improved supplies of food. Later in the nineteenth century health, hygiene and medical advances had a major impact.

However, the birth rate remained high for a number of reasons. Children could work from a young age so they were a source of income and labour. Before the medical improvements of the nineteenth century the **infant mortality** rate was very high so parents wanted a large family to make sure that at least some would survive. Also, methods of **contraception** were not widely available.

In stage three the birth rate began to fall. Child labour was stopped. Parents gained confidence in the ability of new medicine to keep their children alive. Methods of contraception became more widely available.

We are now in stage four. Most parents want to spend their money on other things as well as children, and women, on average, are starting families later in their lives. As a result, the birth rate has stayed low and our population total is relatively stable.

Population change in India

In comparison with England and Wales, India has a high rate of population increase. In 1981 India's population was 684 million. In 1991 it was 882 million. By 2035 it could be more than 2000 million. India is a poor country and it is having problems coping with all these extra people.

Its birth rate is high for four main reasons:

● children can leave school when they are 11 and work on the farm or earn money for the family;
● parents want someone to look after them when they are old because very few people get a pension;
● parents do not believe that modern medicine will keep their children alive (not so long ago many children died);
● it is difficult to get hold of contraceptives.

Its death rate has gone down because medicine is so much better than it used to be, and because food is generally in better supply.

The Indian Government has tried to do something about this situation. India was one of the first **LEDCs** to have a **family planning** policy. In the 1960s the Government tried to explain to parents why it was a good idea to have a smaller family but they could not get their message across. Next, it tried to encourage parents to be **sterilised** by offering money and free gifts but this did not work either. It then tried to force people to be sterilised by stopping their wages but this was very unpopular. Now, they have gone back to encouraging parents to have smaller families: this time they have been more successful (the number of parents using contraceptives has gone up from 4 per cent to 25 per cent) but this is still not good enough.

Fig 11   Spreading the message: an Indian coin

1 Draw a bar chart to show the growth in India's population.
2 Use the statistics in Fig 12 to draw a line graph to show India's changing birth and death rates since 1880. Describe the changes which have taken place.
3 Which stage of the demographic transition do you think India is in? Explain your answer.
4 Why has India's birth rate stayed high? Compare these reasons with stage three of the demographic transition in England and Wales.
5 Why has India's death rate fallen? Compare these reasons with stage three of the demographic transition in England and Wales.
6 Why do you think forcing people to be sterilised was unpopular?
7 How successful has India's family planning policy been?
8 Why do you think people in the UK and India have different attitudes about population and birth control?

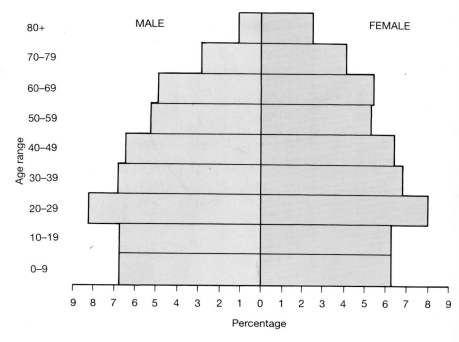

Fig 13 UK's age-sex pyramid

Young or old – does it matter?

The best way of showing the **age structure** of a population is with a special type of bar graph known as an age-sex or population pyramid. The population is divided into five or ten year age groups and the graph is divided into two halves with the left hand side for males and the right hand side for females. Each bar of the graph shows the number of males or females in that age group expressed as a percentage of the total population. Fig 13 shows you the UK's age-sex pyramid while Fig 14 gives you the statistics you need for drawing India's age-sex pyramid.

Age group	% males	% females
0–9	13	12.75
10–19	11.50	10.75
20–29	9	8
30–39	6	6.25
40–49	5	4.50
50–59	3.50	3.25
60–69	2	2
70–79	0.75	1
80+	0.25	0.50

Fig 14 Statistics for India's age-sex pyramid

YEAR	1880	1890	1900	1910	1920	1930	1940	1950	1960	1970	1980	1990
BR	48	41	51	46	38	45	43	40	38	37	34	30
DR	40	43	53	39	40	38	36	31	20	16	12	10

Fig 12 India's changing birth and death rates 1880–1990

MEDCs generally have a population pyramid that looks like the UK's. This is what you would expect when birth and death rates are relatively low. In comparison, the population pyramids of LEDCs are generally like India's because of their high birth and death rates.

Population pyramids also give us an indication of the **dependent** (non-working) and **working populations** of a place, region or country because two major groups of dependants can be identified, the young and the elderly. However, this is only an indication because, for example, in the UK young people can start full-time work at the age of 16 years whereas in India most young people start work before this.

Fig 15   Dependent population

Fig 16   Working population

ENQUIRY

1   Draw an age-sex pyramid for India using the statistics in Fig 14.
2   Compare the percentage of under 10s in the UK and India. Mention similarities as well as differences, and try to explain them.
3   Compare the percentage of over 60s in the UK and India. Mention similarities as well as differences, and try to explain them.
For the following questions take the dependent population to be the percentage of people in the 0-9 age group and the percentage of people in the 60-69 age group and above.
4   What percentage of India's population is dependent?
5   What percentage of UK's population is dependent?
6   In what ways are the dependent populations of India and the UK different?

7   What do the working populations of each of these countries need to provide for their dependent populations? Are there any differences, and if so, why?
8   Why is it easier for the UK to support a dependent population than it is for India to support one? (The income figures on page 147 should help you with this answer.)
9   If India's birth rate stays the same or increases what will happen to the shape of her population pyramid when the present 0-9 age group starts having children? Explain your answer.
10   If the UK's birth rate was to fall and stay at a much lower level what would the consequences be in 20 or 40 years time?
11   What are the problems with the definitions of dependent population used in your answers to the above questions?

1.3 Why do we keep moving around?

Types of movement

People do not keep still! We are always on the move, over long and short distances and for different lengths of time. The many types of movement can be put into different categories.

1 The journey to work. As transport has improved, the distance people travel to work has increased. Someone who travels to another settlement to work, or from one part of a city to another, is known as a **commuter**. For example, 500 000 commuters work in the City of London and some travel from as far away as Peterborough and Brighton. Commuting brings with it the problem of the rush hour which is discussed in Section 2.7.

2 Migration. This is when people move home. Migrations are divided up according to how far people have moved and where they have come from. Some of the main types of migration are:

a) local migration. Moving house to the next street along is an example of a local migration. In this chapter, take any migration of 20 km or less to be a local migration.

b) rural-urban migration. This is a movement from the countryside to the town (see Section 2.8).

c) urban-rural migration. This is movement from the town to the countryside (see Section 2.7).

d) guest-worker migration. Guest-workers leave their country to work in another. Most are male and they usually leave their families behind. They send as much of their money as they can, back home. Most have to return to their own country after a certain period of time.

e) international migration. Millions of people have left their own country to live permanently in another. When you leave a country you are an emigrant. When you settle in a new country you are an immigrant.

ENQUIRY

1 List and briefly define, the types of movement described on this page.

2 Carry out a 'journey to work' survey. You could interview people yourself, or you could organise it as a class survey. The ideas on page 16 should help.

3 What is the difference between an immigrant and an emigrant?

4 Have you ever migrated? If you have, where did you migrate from and to? What was the reason for your migration (e.g. job, family reason)? Read through the information about migration again and decide which type of migration yours was. Show the route of your migration on a suitable map. How far did you migrate? (NB If you have migrated more than once treat each migration separately. If you haven't migrated find someone who has and do this exercise for them!)

Fig 17   The rush hour

The journey to work

Name	Address	Place of work	Distance travelled	Method of transport

Fig 18 Journey to work questionnaire

JOURNEY TO WORK SURVEY

Aim of Survey   To find out about people's journey to work.

Method   Interview at least 20 people using a questionnaire like the one in Fig 18.

Presentation of results

a) Home address and place of work. Mark these onto a base map. The two places can then be joined by a straight line. An arrow should show the direction of movement.

b) Distance travelled. The number of people in each of the following 'distance categories' could be shown as a bar graph: 0-2.9 km; 3-5.9 km; 6-8.9 km; 9-11.9 km; 12-14.9 km; 15 km and above.

c) Method of Transport. This could be shown as a bar graph. Alternatively, this information could be added to the 'distance travelled' graph by shading in each 'distance travelled category' in order to show how the people in that category get to work.

Conclusion   Here are some questions you could try to answer as part of your conclusion.
Is there a pattern to where people work?
Do people who travel short distances to work use a different method of transport to those who travel long distances?
How many of the people in your survey are commuters?

Changing distributions in the UK

Fig 19 shows that since 1981 the population of some parts of the country has gone up while in other parts it has gone down. This is mainly because of people migrating from one place to another. Many reasons help to explain why this has happened but one of the most important is the decline of jobs in the north of the country and the growth of jobs in the south of the country (see Section 3.3).

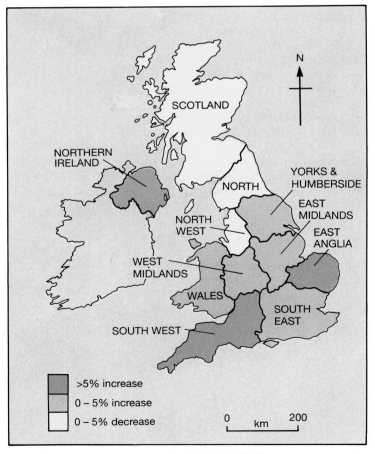

Fig 19 Population change in the UK 1981-1991

Where people would like to live – **residential preference** – is another factor which helps to explain changing distributions. For example, many people move when they retire and the seaside towns on the south coast are a popular destination; this can be seen in the population structures in Fig 20. Your own residential preference can be explored through the survey on page 18.

Changes have taken place within regions as well. Fig 21 shows population change in the south east planning region between 1981 and 1991. Throughout the country many millions of people have been leaving large towns and cities in search of better housing, a nicer environment and new jobs. Also, better transport has made it possible for more people to commute to work in the city from dormitory settlements in the countryside. These ideas are explored again in Section 2.7.

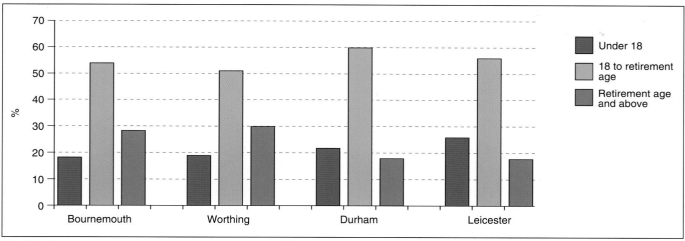

Fig 20 Population structures of selected districts, 1991

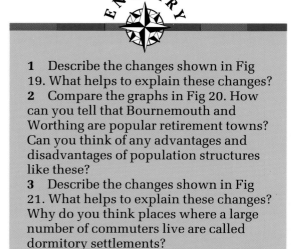

1   Describe the changes shown in Fig 19. What helps to explain these changes?
2   Compare the graphs in Fig 20. How can you tell that Bournemouth and Worthing are popular retirement towns? Can you think of any advantages and disadvantages of population structures like these?
3   Describe the changes shown in Fig 21. What helps to explain these changes? Why do you think places where a large number of commuters live are called dormitory settlements?

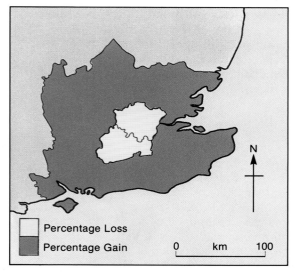

Percentage Loss

Percentage Gain

0   km   100

Fig 21 Population change, south east planning region 1981-1991

RESIDENTIAL PREFERENCE SURVEY

Aim To find out where you would and would not like to live in the UK.

Method Find each of the regions in Fig 22 in an atlas in order to see what they are like, e.g. are they mountainous, or do they have a lot of big towns and cities? Then, give each region a score on the following scale:

3 = you would like to live there
2 = you wouldn't mind living there
1 = you wouldn't like to live there

Presentation of Results On a copy of Fig 22 shade in each region according to the score you have given it. Use the key suggested on the map.

Conclusion Here are some questions you could answer as part of your conclusion. Is there a pattern on your map? What do you think explains the regions you would like to live in, e.g. are they places you have lived in before, or places you have been to on holiday? What explains the regions you would not like to live in – are they regions you know very little about, or are they regions with a lot of big towns and cities? Compare your map with someone else's and try to explain any similarities and differences.

Patterns of Migration in the European Union

The period since 1945 has seen a large-scale migration of people from (mainly) southern Europe, North Africa, the Caribbean, Asia and (more recently) eastern Europe, to the north and west of Europe.

At least 13 million people have migrated permanently and many more guest-workers have migrated temporarily. Germany, France and the UK have, between them, received most of these migrants but other countries have received significant numbers as well (Fig 23).

Migration can be seen in terms of **push factors** – ones which force you to move from a place – and **pull factors** – ones which attract you to a place. The pull of jobs in the expanding economies of the industrialised countries of north and west Europe was the main reason for the migration of the 1950s and 1960s. The migrants were recruited to do 'dirty' jobs, like refuse disposal, but they could still earn much more than at home.

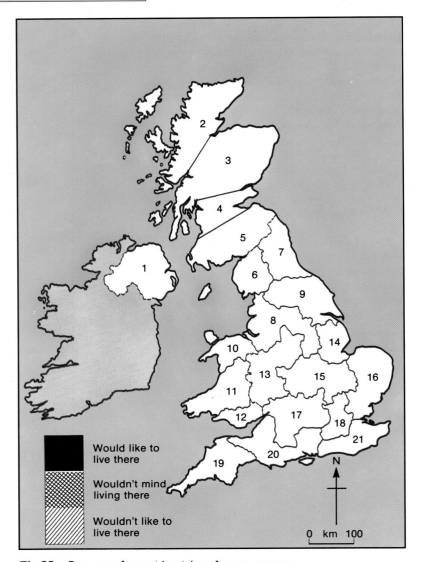

Fig 22 Base map for residential preference survey

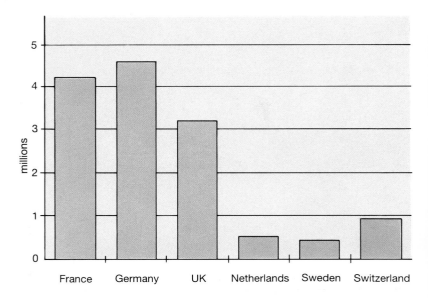

Fig 23 The number of foreign migrants in selected countries

The consequences of these migrations have been both positive and negative. For example, on the one hand the economies of the host countries have benefited from a supply of cheap labour, but on the other, there have been outbreaks of racial violence. These, and other ideas, are explored more fully in the following case studies.

Migration in Germany

Germany has received more migrants since 1945 than any other EU country. In the 1950s and 1960s guest-workers were recruited, first from southern Italy and then from Yugoslavia, Greece and Turkey (Fig 24). They were given short-term contracts and were not expected to settle permanently.

In 1973 a serious **economic recession** began to affect the EU. Germany immediately cut back on its recruitment of foreign workers, although the total number of migrants continued to rise (Fig 25). This was mainly because changes in policy had made it easier for guest-workers to settle permanently and they were being joined by their wives and families.

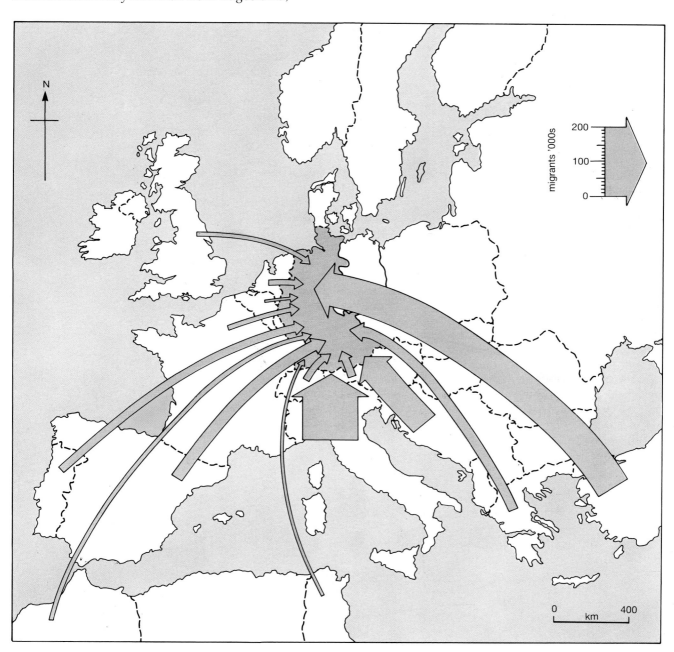

Fig 24   Origin and number of guest workers 1972

By 1983 migrants accounted for 7.5 per cent of the total population, the largest group being of Turkish origin. However, their distribution within the country, and within towns and cities, was uneven (Fig 26).

At the end of the 1980s the collapse of communism in eastern Europe meant that restrictions on movement were lifted and this led to a new wave of migration. In the two years 1989 and 1990 Germany received nearly one million migrants. Most of these were **ethnic** Germans who had found themselves living in other countries when the map of Europe was re-drawn at the end of the Second World War; as such, they had a guaranteed right to German citizenship.

These migrations have had many consequences. During the 1950s and 1960s Germany's economy undoubtedly benefited from the supply of cheap labour. For example, studies have shown that guest-workers produced more goods and services than they consumed.

However, when unemployment rose in the 1970s, and again in the 1980s, the jobless rate for immigrants was higher than average, so they cost the government relatively more in social security benefits. Coping with the recent migrants from eastern Europe has been particularly expensive because the overwhelming majority arrived with no job, nowhere to live, no money and few possessions.

Housing problems have resulted from the relatively low wages earnt by the migrants because they have had no choice but to live in the poorest districts. Run-down, overcrowded housing causes health problems and contributes towards a low standard of living.

Integration – fitting in – has been a problem for many of the migrants because they have their own languages, religions and cultures; e.g. 1.7 million of Germany's migrants are Muslims, mainly from Turkey. One consequence has been urban **segregation**, with immigrants living in separate areas of towns and cities. Also, 'being different' has made them the focus of **racial prejudice**.

Age structure is another problem. This is because the immigrant population has a higher birth rate than the German population, so it has a larger percentage of young people. The government has to pay for their education and welfare and find employment for them when they leave school.

The German Government's policy for dealing with these problems has three main aspects:

- **Integration.** This is aimed largely at the children of the immigrants, most of whom would like to fit in more with German society. It involves, for example, language training and information campaigns.
- **Restrictions on entry.** These are designed to keep down the number of new migrants. For example, it has become more difficult for children over the age of 16 to join their parents.
- **Voluntary repatriation.** This involves encouraging migrants to return home by offering them special payments. However, most would prefer to stay in Germany where conditions are better whether they have a job or not.

These policies have had some success but Germany's current economic difficulties, resulting largely from the cost of re-unification with East Germany, have once again made its immigrant population the focus of racial attacks (Fig 27). Few people had expected these problems in the boom years of the 1950s and 1960s.

Fig 25   Foreign workers and the foreign population 1974-1982

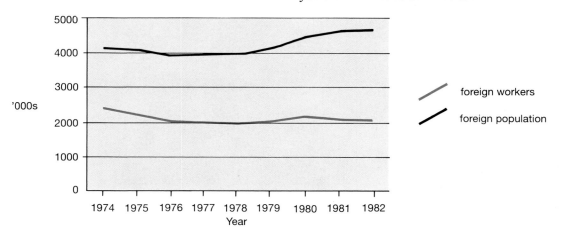

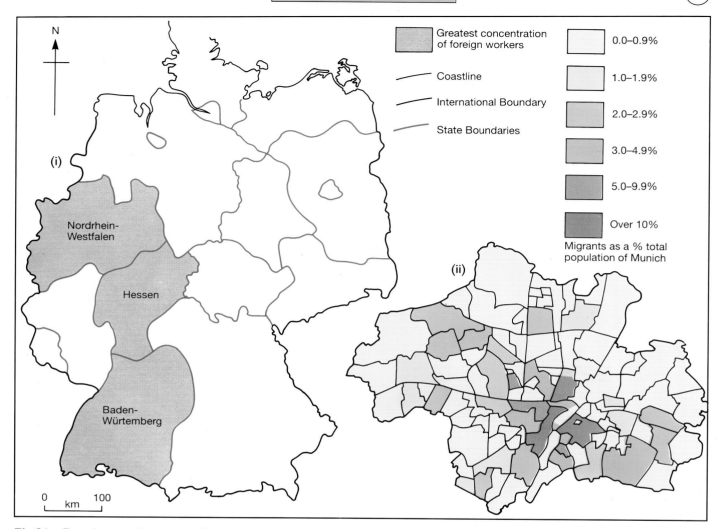

Fig 26   Distribution of migrants   (i) In Germany   (ii) In Munich

Fig 27   Racial incident, Germany

Migration in Spain

Spain is one of the countries of southern Europe which has seen large-scale emigration. In the 1960s at least one million Spaniards left for other European countries, particularly France and Germany. The main pull factor was the chance of a better paid job. The main push factor was the decline in rural employment as Spain changed from a traditional society based on labour-intensive farming to a more modern industrial society.

This migration had its advantages; for example, it kept down the level of unemployment, and the money sent home by the migrants was the country's second most important source of foreign revenue, after tourism. However, it had its disadvantages as well; for example, it took young and active people away at a time when the modernisation process needed energy and enthusiasm.

The recession of the 1970s saw the return of many of these migrants, so that by 1981 less than 350 000 Spaniards were living in north and west Europe (Fig 28). This brought its young people back but it boosted the unemployment total, and reduced an important source of foreign revenue.

It can be seen from these case studies that migration in Europe since 1945 can be divided into three main periods:

● **The 1950s and 1960s.** In this period, workers from the poorer south were encouraged to migrate to the richer north to fill job vacancies.
● **The 1970s and 1980s.** In this period, economic recession saw an end to the recruitment of workers but foreign populations continued to rise as earlier migrants were joined by their families.
● **The late 1980s.** More recently, there has been a big increase in the number of migrants from eastern Europe.

During this time, policy towards migrants has changed. The encouragement given in the 1950s and 1960s gave way to discouragement in the 1970s. In the 1980s the countries which had received substantial numbers of migrants adopted a variety of strategies, some of which were designed to stop further immigration (e.g. treating illegal immigration harshly) and some of which were designed to help the migrants who were already settled (e.g. integration programmes).

More recently, the EU has started to discuss a common policy towards migration. The first of its main aims is to remove restrictions on movement within its borders: this could result in a new wave of internal migration but only if some economics become much stronger than others. The second is to agree a common approach towards immigration into the Union: it has been suggested that countries use the same procedures for processing applications and that they work together on patrolling the Union's land and sea borders.

In the short-term, continued pressure from eastern Europe is likely to be the most significant trend; for example, it has been estimated that there are as many as 20 million potential migrants from the former USSR. The main push factors are economic, e.g. high unemployment rates and low wages, although political persecution and, increasingly, civil wars, are forcing people to migrate as well. It has also been estimated that there are as many as 500 000 potential migrants a year from LEDCs.

The EU is likely to put up tough barriers in an attempt to control these potential migrants. However, it has been argued that some migration should be allowed because the EU's population is falling and there could be shortages in certain areas of employment.

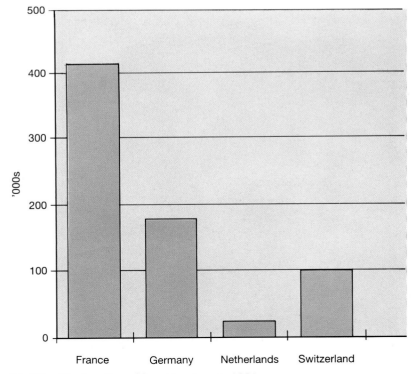

Fig 28 The location of Spanish migrants 1981

ENQUIRY

1 What has been the overall pattern of migration in Europe since 1945 and how many people have been involved?

2 Explain what is meant by push and pull factors. What was the main pull factor in the migrations of the 1950s and 1960s?

3 Describe and explain the pattern of migration shown on Fig 24.

4 Describe and explain the trends shown on Fig 25.

5 Compare Fig 26 (i) with a map showing the distribution of industry and population in Germany. What do you notice about the areas with the greatest concentration of migrants?

6 Describe and explain the distribution of migrant workers in Munich.

7 Where have Germany's most recent migrants come from, and why?

8 Make a list of the advantages and disadvantages to Germany of these various migrations.

9 Describe, in detail, two of the problems Germany has had to deal with.

10 In general, how has the German Government tried to deal with the consequences of migration, and how successful has it been?

11 Why did so many people leave Spain in the 1960s?

12 What were the advantages and disadvantages to Spain of these various migrations?

13 Describe and explain the three stages of migration to the EU shown on Fig 29. What was the Government policy in each of these stages?

14 Where are most migrants to the EU likely to come from in the next ten years, and why? What are the arguments for and against letting these migrants into the Community? What is the EU likely to do, and what do you think it should do?

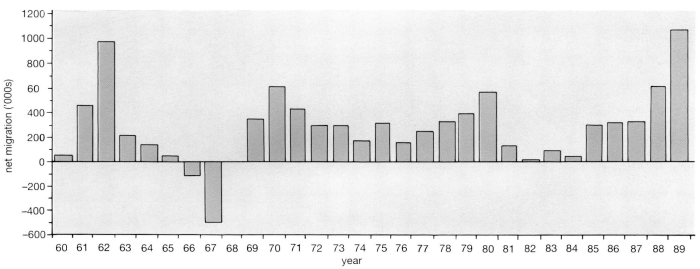

Fig 29 Migration to the EU 1960-1989

1.4 Assessment task: *Population and migration in the USA*

When Columbus reached the New World in 1492 it is estimated that there were two million American Indians living in what is now the USA, with a density of 0.2 people per square kilometre. Five hundred years of immigration and natural increase have seen the population of the USA rise to 256 million and its density increase to 27 people per square kilometre. Its population distribution is shown in Fig 30.

Immigrants to the USA have come from many different parts of the world. One consequence of this is that its population is made up of different ethnic groups – people who share the same history, and/or language, and/or culture (Fig 31).

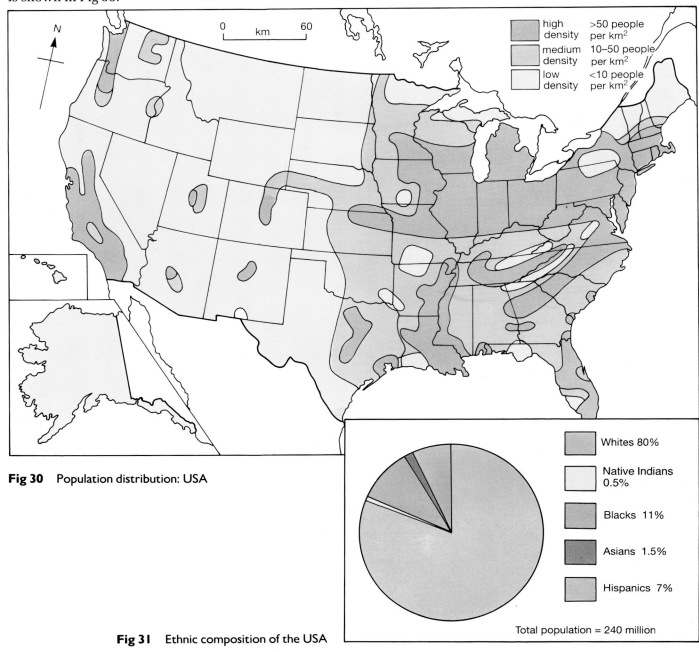

Fig 30   Population distribution: USA

Legend:
- high density   >50 people per km²
- medium density   10–50 people per km²
- low density   <10 people per km²

Pie chart legend:
- Whites 80%
- Native Indians 0.5%
- Blacks 11%
- Asians 1.5%
- Hispanics 7%

Total population = 240 million

Fig 31   Ethnic composition of the USA

Until 1945 Europeans dominated immigration (Fig 32). Before 1890, most came from Britain, Ireland, Germany and Scandinavia, but after 1890 most came from Poland, Russia and Italy. Some, like the Pilgrim Fathers, came in search of greater freedom; most came in search of work.

Since 1945, Hispanics (Spanish-speaking peoples from Mexico, Puerto Rico and Cuba) and Asians (from China, the Philippines, Japan and South East Asia) have been the main immigrant groups (Fig 32); for most of these, the pull of employment has been the principal reason for migrating, although for some (e.g. Cubans and Cambodians) push factors have been important because they have fled from hostile governments.

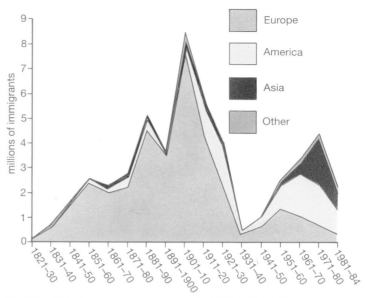

Fig 32 Main immigrant groups to the USA 1821-1984

numbers and today they total only 1.5 million. Most live on the reservations in the south west which were set up at the end of the Indian Wars in 1890 (Fig 33).

The majority of Black Americans are the descendants of slaves taken from Africa to the southern States in the seventeenth, eighteenth and nineteenth centuries. Slavery was abolished at the end of the Civil War in 1865 but most Blacks continued to work and live on the tobacco and cotton plantations for low wages and in very poor conditions (Fig 34). However, a major change took place between 1920 and 1940 when many of them migrated to the cities of the Manufacturing Belt in the north of the country, attracted by the demand for factory workers.

Fig 33 Navajo family, Winslow in Arizona

The Native Indians used to live in all parts of the country, as subsistence farmers and/or hunters and gatherers. However, conflict with European settlers dramatically reduced their

Fig 34 Tobacco plantation near Jonesville, Virginia

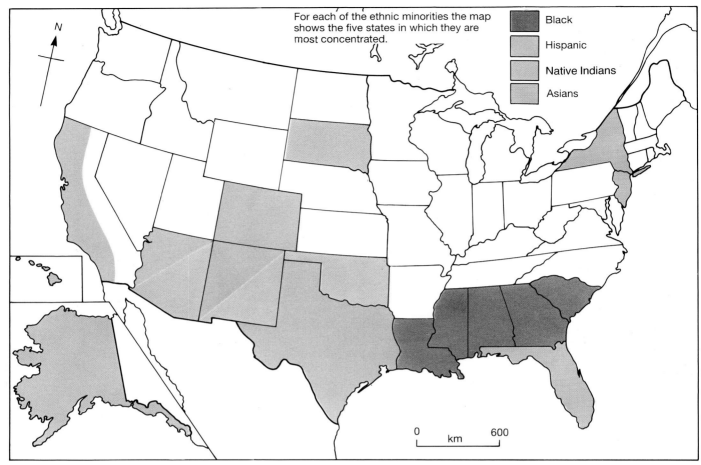

Fig 35 The distribution of ethnic minorities in the USA

A more recent trend has been a movement of people from the Manufacturing Belt in the north of the country to the Sunbelt states in the south of the country (Fig 36). This has happened because of the decline of traditional manufacturing industry in the north and the expansion of **light and high-technology industry** in the south; and because of the attractions of the warmer climate and pleasanter environment in the south (see Section 3.8).

The USA has often been described as a racial 'melting pot' but there has been little integration between the main ethnic groups. This can be seen in the uneven distribution of the minority groups (Fig 35).

Also, with the exception of the Native Indians and the southern Blacks, the ethnic minorities live in urban, rather than rural, areas. The main explanation for this is the greater number and range of job opportunities to be found in cities but 'safety in numbers' is also important i.e. it is easier for a sizeable community, which can provide support and self-help, to develop in a city.

The USA's ethnic diversity has had a number of consequences. The minority groups have been subject to official and unofficial discrimination. Until the Civil Rights movement of the 1960s, laws denied Blacks equal access to housing, jobs and education. Official barriers have now been removed but unofficial ones still operate which make progress difficult.

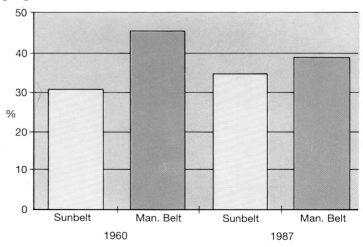

Fig 36 Population change: Manufacturing Belt vs Sunbelt

Blacks are significantly worse off than Whites against a whole range of social and economic indicators (Fig 37). Black ghettos have developed in the run-down inner cities because these are the only areas in which the majority can afford to live (Fig 38).

Some Blacks have been able to move to the suburbs. However, the number has been small (only 14 per cent in 1984) and, with the development of Black suburbs, segregation has continued.

The consequences of Hispanic migration could be even more far reaching. They are the fastest growing group in the USA today, not only because of immigration but also because of a much higher than average birth rate. If their current growth rate continues they could become the largest of all the ethnic groups – including Whites – within a generation. The large number of Mexicans in California has already led to official recognition that the State is bilingual; e.g. the instructions on how to use a public telephone in Los Angeles have been written in Spanish as well as English since the early 1980s.

	BLACKS	WHITES
median income (US $ 1982)	13 598	24 603
% of families below poverty line (1983)	32.4	9.7
total value of possessions for the average household (US $)	26 608	68 891
unemployment rate	consistently double the rate for Whites	
births to teenagers per 1000	515	225

Fig 37 Socio-economic indicators: Blacks vs Whites

Fig 38 Lower East Side, Manhattan in New York

In 1992, two police officers in Los Angeles were found not guilty of unlawfully beating up Rodney King, a Black man who had been arrested for a traffic offence. The original incident had been widely publicised because it had been filmed by a passer-by with a video recorder and was shown on television. The verdict triggered the worst riots in the country's history: a graphic illustration of what the consequences of ethnic diversity can be (Fig 39).

Pressure from would-be migrants looks set to continue. In 1990, one million Mexicans were caught trying to enter the USA illegally and it is likely that as many again got in without being stopped. The goverment deports (returns) illegal immigrants straight away but at the same time it has a policy of encouraging highly skilled professionals; e.g. in 1990 it tripled the number of visas given to such people, to 140 000.

Fig 39   Los Angeles riots, 30 April 1992

Task

1   With the help of an atlas, describe and explain the distribution of population in the USA.

2   Describe and explain the movement of Blacks from south to north between 1920 and 1940, and the more recent movement of people from the Manufacturing Belt to the Sunbelt.

3   Use the information in Fig 40 to help you explain why so many Mexicans wish to migrate to the USA.

4   Describe and explain the main reasons for immigration to the USA since 1945.

5   Describe and explain the distribution of ethnic minorities in the USA. What have the main consequences of ethnic diversity in the USA been?

	USA	MEXICO
Population (millions)	249	88.6
Natural rate of population increase (%)	0.9	2.3
Infant mortality (deaths before age 1, per 1000 births)	8	36
GNP (per person, US $ millions)	21 100	1990
Telephones (per 100 people)	70	10
Food supply (calories per person per day)	3644	3123

Fig 40   Socio-economic indicators: USA vs Mexico

SETTLEMENT

2.1 What type of settlement do I live in?

A **settlement** is a place where people live. It can be either temporary (which means it is only there for a short while) or permanent (which means that it has been built to last).

Fig 41 Is it a settlement?

(i) A village post office

(ii) Desert nomads

(iii) A semi-detached house

(iv) A factory estate

One way of putting settlements into different groups is to say whether they are *rural* or *urban*. Rural settlements are found in the countryside; for example, a village. Urban settlements are built-up areas such as towns and cities.

SETTLEMENT

Another way is to put settlements into a **hierarchy** according to their population and the number of services (e.g. shops, schools and cinemas) they have (Fig 43):

- a *hamlet* has only a few houses and no more than 100 people. It might have one or two services, such as a church and a pub, or it might have none at all;
- a *village*, as a rough guide, has between 101 and 2000 people. It has a number of basic services; e.g. a butchers, a grocers, a bakers, a primary school and possibly a doctor's surgery;
- a *town* is the next largest settlement and it has between 2001 and 100 000 people. As the size of the town increases the number of services also increases. Large towns have big supermarkets, secondary schools, cinemas and usually railway and bus stations;
- **city** is an official title given to a settlement by the King or Queen. However, geographers take a city to be a settlement with 100 001 to 1 000 000 people and a wide range of services including government offices and main train and bus stations;

- a **conurbation** is a large area of urban development. It has a population of between 1 000 001 and 10 000 000 and is the result of towns and cities spreading outwards and joining together. Fig 44 shows Britain's main conurbations;
- finally, a **megalopolis** is a 'super conurbation' which is the result of towns, cities and conurbations joining together.

We can also look at the shape settlements make on a map or an aerial photograph. The main shapes into which settlements can be grouped are shown in Fig 45.

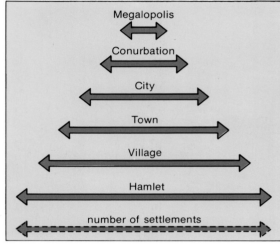

Fig 43　The settlement hierarchy

(i) Rural settlement

Fig 42　What type of settlement?

(ii) Urban settlement

Conurbation	Main towns	Population 1991 (millions)
Greater London	London	6.38
Greater Manchester	Manchester	2.45
West Midlands	Birmingham	2.50
West Yorkshire	Leeds, Bradford	1.98
Clydeside	Glasgow	1.04
Merseyside	Liverpool	1.38
Tyneside	Newcastle	1.09

Fig 44 Britain's main conurbations

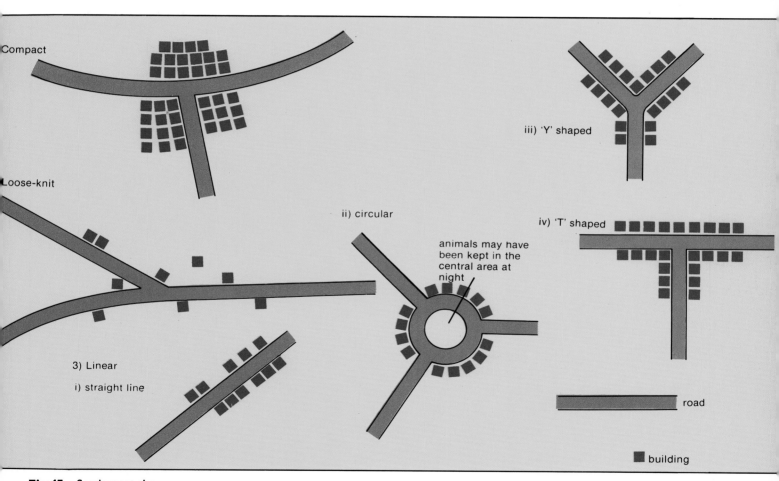

Fig 45 Settlement shapes

In a **compact** or **nucleated** settlement the buildings are close together. This type of settlement may have developed because of the relief of the land, or the need for defence, or because the settlers wished to live in a close community.

A **loose-knit** settlement could be the result of a long period of slow growth with buildings being added on, as and when they are needed.

The different types of **linear** settlement could be the result of the relief of the land or because the buildings have grown up alongside a road, river or canal.

Scale 1:50 000

Ordnance Survey OS

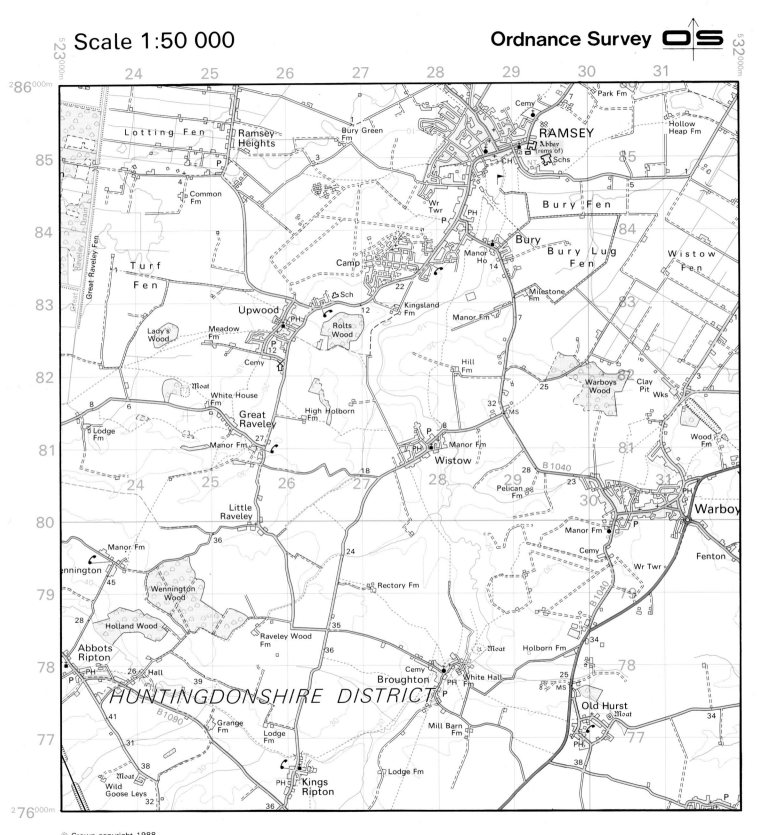

Fig 46 Ordnance Survey map extract reproduced with the permission of the Controller of Her Majesty's Stationery Office, © Crown copyright

ENQUIRY

1 For each of the photographs in Fig 41 decide whether or not it is a settlement. Explain your decision.

2 Write down a list of all the differences you can think of between a rural settlement and an urban settlement: Fig 42 should give you some ideas. Discuss your list in groups of three or four and try to agree on what you think the five most important differences are.

3 Explain, with the help of a diagram, what is meant by the settlement hierarchy.

4 Find out the population of your settlement. Where does it fit into the hierarchy?

5 Try to give an example of each level of the hierarchy from your home region.

6 What happens to the number of settlements as you go up the hierarchy? Try to explain your answer.

7 On an outline map of Britain mark on and label the main conurbations (Fig 44). If they were to carry on growing, which ones might join up to form a megalopolis?

8 In your atlas find a map of the USA. The biggest megalopolis in the world stretches from Boston to Washington DC and includes New York, Philadelphia and Baltimore. It is an almost continuous belt of urban development with a population of 46 million. Mark this megalopolis onto a base map of the USA and write a brief description next to it. What is the distance from Boston to Washington DC? How does this compare with the distance from London to Belfast?

9 Copy and label the diagrams in Fig 45. Under each settlement shape, list the reasons that could explain it. Then, look at the map extract on Fig 46 and for each of the following settlements write down which shape you think it is most like. Also, write down any evidence you can find from the map that might help to explain its shape:

Fig 47 Satellite image of Greater London (i) image

KEY
Red = vegetation
Blue = built-up area
Dark blue/black = water

(ii) base map

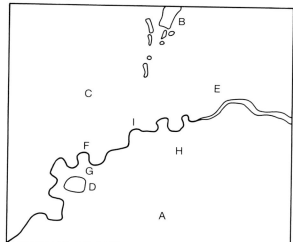

a) Broughton; (28 78)
b) Wistow; (28 81)
c) Abbots Ripton; (23 78)
d) Ramsey Heights; (25 85)
e) Oldhurst; (30 77)
f) Kings Ripton. (26 76)

10 Find a detailed map of London (e.g. in a road atlas) and compare it with Fig 47. Match the letters with the following features/places: River Thames, Lea Valley, Richmond Park, Lewisham, Croydon, Putney, Hammersmith, Hendon, Ilford.

2.2 How does a village grow and develop?

Brampton is a village in Cambridgeshire which has seen a big increase in its population in the last 50 years (Fig 48). Its **site** – the land upon which it is built – is an area of slightly higher ground above the flood plains of Alconbury Brook and the River Great Ouse, and it is **situated** close to the A1, within easy reach of the railway station in Huntingdon (Fig 49).

Very little is known about the earliest settlers in Brampton, although Iron Age farms, 2500 years old, have been found nearby. The village was probably built by the Saxons, who moved into the area 1500 years ago, because its name is a Saxon word meaning 'bramble clearing'. However, the first time Brampton is mentioned in a written record is in the Domesday Book of 1086 (Fig 50). This tells us that it was a farming settlement. Cows for milk and meat were grazed on the flood plain, and crops were grown on the drier ground away from the river.

The growth and development of the village is shown in Fig 51. The oldest surviving building is St Mary's church, parts of which date back to the thirteenth century. There are also a number of seventeenth century buildings, such as Pepys Cottage, The Black Bull, and some of the cottages along the High Street.

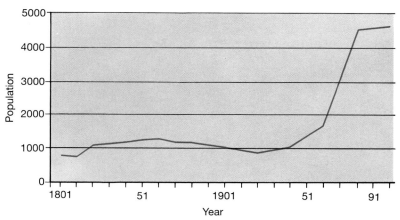

Fig 48 Brampton's population growth

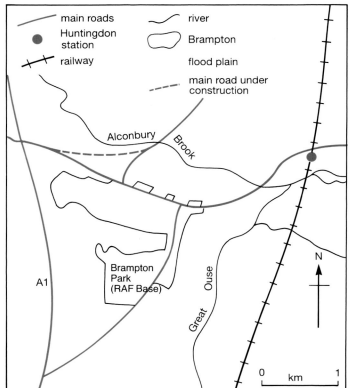

Fig 49 Brampton's site and situation

LAND OF THE KING

In Brampton King Edward had 15 hides taxable. Land for 15 ploughs. Now 3 ploughs there. 36 villagers and 2 smallholders have 14 ploughs. A church and a priest. Meadow, 100 acres; woodland pasture half a league long and 2 furlongs wide; 2 mills which pay 100s. Value before 1066 and now £20. Ranulf brother of Ilger has charge of it.

LAND OF THE KING'S THANES

In Brampton Alric, 1 hide and 1 virgate of land taxable. Land for 10 oxen. 3 smallholders; 1 plough. Value 30s.

Fig 50 An extract from the Domesday Book

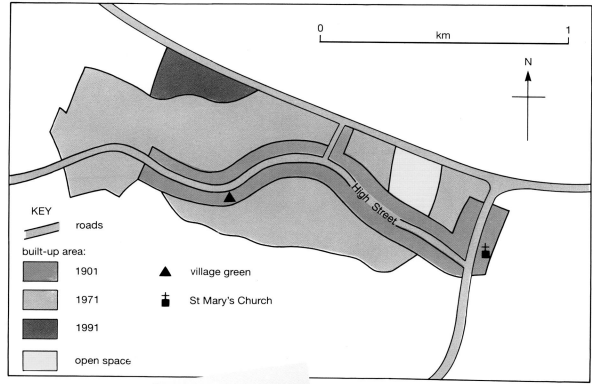

Fig 51 The growth and development of Brampton

KEY

roads

built-up area:

1901

1971

1991

open space

▲ village green

✝ St Mary's Church

Fig 52 The Black Bull

Fig 53 RAF Brampton

The triangular shape of the village green suggests that it may have been used for archery practice in medieval times.

In the eighteenth century, the Great North Road – now the A1 – became important for coach travel between London and the north of the country. It passed very close to Brampton and this helped the development of the village because travellers used it as a place to stay overnight on their journeys. One of the coaching inns, at the roundabout to the west of the village, was known as Creamer's Hut, after the man who owned it; part of this name has survived to the present day with the roundabout being known as Brampton Hut.

Brampton Park has played an important part in the history of the village. It goes back to the twelfth century, and a number of important families have owned it and lived there. It was taken over by the Air Force in 1939 and it has been developed into a large and important RAF base (Fig 53). Many families live on the base and more live in the village itself.

Brampton has also become an important **dormitory settlement** – a place where people live but travel to work (commute) somewhere else. This has been made possible by the improvements in transport in recent years. It takes only an hour to get to London from Huntingdon by train and the A1 is a good, fast road.

New estates have been built, mainly to the west and south of the old village, to house the people who have moved to Brampton since 1941 (Fig 54). Houses have also been built on empty land between buildings in the old village: these are known as infill sites (Fig 55). More new housing is under construction, or has been planned (Fig 56).

Fig 54　New houses

Fig 55　Infill site

ENQUIRY

1　Why would Brampton have been a good site for a Saxon settlement?
2　What are the advantages of Brampton's situation?
3　The numbers in the Domesday survey are in family units e.g. ten villagers or smallholders means ten families. How many family units are mentioned in the extract? If each family had five people what, roughly, was Brampton's population in 1086?
4　Draw and label a sketch map to show the main stages in the growth and development of Brampton.
5　Why has Brampton's population gone up so dramatically since 1941?
6　What could **a)** the good and **b)** the bad effects be on Brampton of the opening of the A1-M1 link?
7　Two areas where future growth could take place in Brampton are shown in Fig 56. What do you think are the advantages and disadvantages of developing each of these areas? Which, on balance, would you choose, and why?

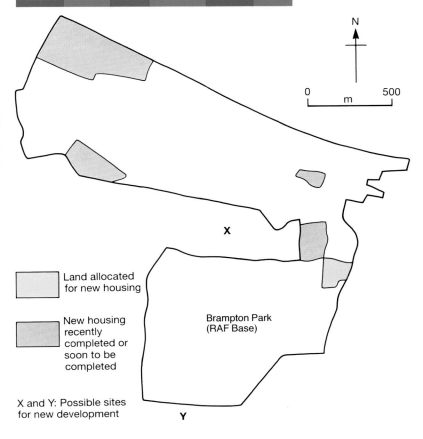

Land allocated for new housing

New housing recently completed or soon to be completed

X and Y: Possible sites for new development

Fig 56　Brampton's development plan

2.3 *Where do we build our settlements?*

It can take a great deal of detective work to find out why a particular site was chosen for a settlement.

Place names can give us clues about who first built a settlement, as well as why they chose that site (Fig 57). However, we have to be careful with this sort of evidence because the name of the settlement might have been changed since it was first built.

Fig 57 Place name evidence

Place name	Meaning	Date		Colour
chester	fort	Roman	(43 AD-410 AD)	black
ing	territory	early Saxon	410 AD	brown
ham	home	early Saxon		brown
ton	enclosure	early Saxon		brown
don	hill	early Saxon		brown
ley	clearing	middle Saxon		red
stow	(holy) place	middle Saxon		red
den	clearing for pigs in a wood	late Saxon		blue
hurst	wood	late Saxon	1066 AD	blue
'French sounding' e.g. D'Arcy	often name of person given to settlement by William the Conqueror	Norman	1066 AD 1150 AD	green
fen	wet place	1600s and 1700s		yellow
mere	wet place	1600s and 1700s		yellow
lake	lake	1600s and 1700s		yellow

The site and situation of a settlement can also give many clues (Fig 58). However, in towns and cities a lot of the evidence is buried under buildings and roads and it can be very difficult to work out what the place used to be like.

ENQUIRY

1 Study an Ordnance Survey map for your area (or the map on page 34). Draw a sketch map to show the distribution of settlement. Label onto the map the name of each settlement. Decide how old it is using place name evidence. (If you have some place names which are not in Fig 57 see what you can find out about them from the local library). Using the colours suggested in Fig 57 put a dot next to each settlement. What is the oldest settlement on your map? How old is your settlement? Is there a pattern to the age of settlements on your map? If there is, describe it and try to explain it. Do the place names on your map give any clues about why those sites were chosen?

2 Which of the settlement locations in Fig 58 are mainly to do with site factors, and which are mainly to do with situation? Are there any examples of these settlement locations on the map you prepared for question 1?

Anglo-Saxon settlers game

When the Romans ended their occupation of Britain around 400 AD a group of people now known as the Anglo-Saxons migrated here from parts of present day Germany. These people arrived by boat in small family groups and many of them sailed inland along rivers. The Anglo-Saxons were farmers, keeping animals and growing crops, and they lived in hamlets and small villages.

Pretend that you are a member of one of these Anglo-Saxon families and that you are looking for a good place to build a settlement. In choosing this place you would have to consider a number of factors:

PHYSICAL FACTORS

a) **dry land** – you would not want to settle in an area that was likely to flood;

b) **water supply** – water is heavy to carry and you would need a good supply not too far from your settlement;

c) **defence** – you would want an easy place to defend because there is no guarantee that the locals are going to be friendly!

d) **shelter** – you would want a sheltered site, especially for the winter;

e) **aspect** – this means which way a settlement is facing. If you decide to settle in a valley the sunny side would be better for crops than the shady side.

ECONOMIC FACTORS

f) **food supply** – you would need to be in a good area for farming;

g) **resources** – e.g. a source of fuel such as wood for burning;

h) **transport and communications** – you would want an easy means of transport, such as a river.

SOCIAL FACTORS

i) **decision-making** – you cannot survive alone: will your group be able to agree on a site or will you have to look for another one?

j) **political** – if people do already live in the area will you be able to come to an agreement with them?

Working in groups of four or five, study the sketch map and sketch in Fig 60. For each of the sites (A to E) agree on a score on the following scale for the physical and economic factors (a to h) listed on this page.

3   if the site is good in this respect;
2   if the site is average in this respect;
1   if the site is poor in this respect.

Set your results out in a table like the one in Fig 59.

When you have finished the scoring study the results and decide which site you would choose for your settlement. Your group must come to an agreement!

Which site did your group choose for your settlement and why? Would your group have liked more information? What extra information would have been helpful? Did the social factors (i) and (j) play a part in your decision? Did the other groups in your class agree or disagree with your group's decision? If there were disagreements what do you think explains them? Which site(s) did your group give the lowest score to? Why?

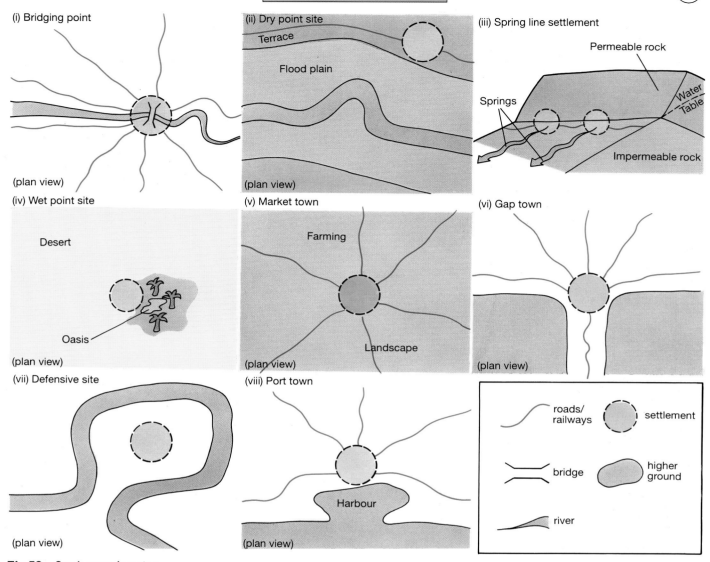

Fig 58 Settlement location

FACTOR	a	b	c	d	e	f	g	h	TOTAL
SITE									
A									
B									
C									
D									
E									

Fig 59 Site score sheet

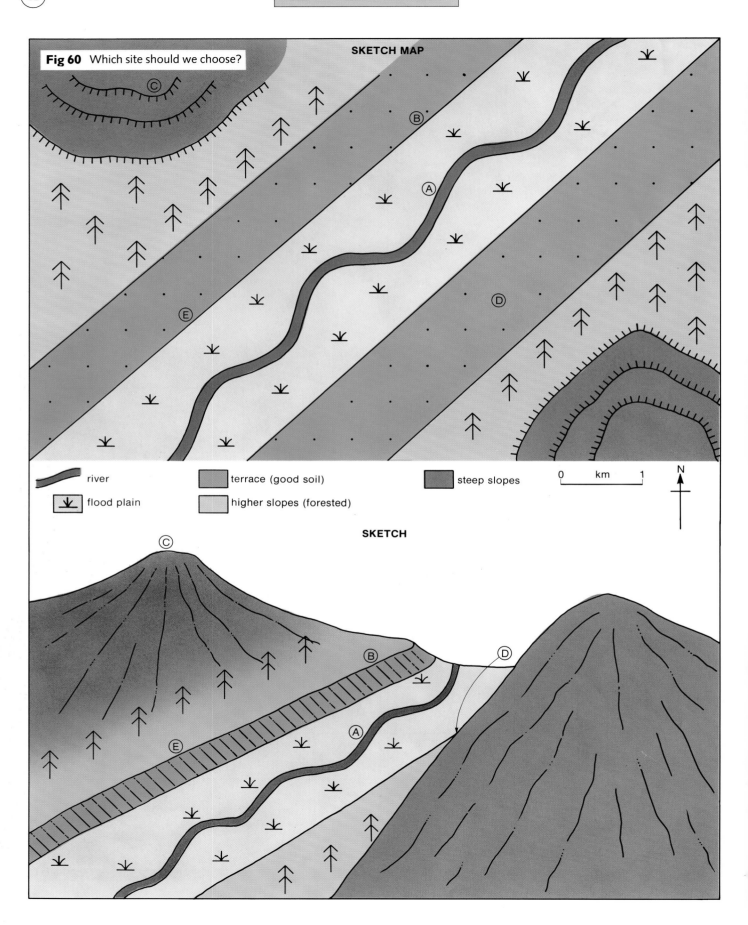

Fig 60 Which site should we choose?

SKETCH MAP

river

flood plain

terrace (good soil)

higher slopes (forested)

steep slopes

0   km   1

N

SKETCH

The growth and development of London

Evidence of human activity in the London area goes back several thousand years. The first permanent settlement was built by the Romans nearly 2000 years ago. They chose the site of the present day City of London where they built a bridge across the Thames. The settlement itself stretched westwards to the River Fleet and was protected by a wall, parts of which can still be seen (Fig 61).

Very little is known about London's history in the years after the Romans left, but people almost certainly carried on living in the settlement they had built. We do know that at the end of the tenth century the Saxons built a cathedral and a royal palace where the City of Westminster is today. This development was followed by the Normans building the Tower of London (Fig 62) shortly after their invasion, although they chose Westminster as their centre of government and began the building of Westminster Abbey (Fig 63). The City of Westminster and the City of London were separated by marshy ground and the only route between them, other than the river, was a narrow causeway known as the Strand; it looks very different today! (Fig 64). It was not until the late seventeenth century that this marshy ground was reclaimed and the two Cities merged together.

Fig 61   Roman wall

Fig 62   Tower of London

Fig 63   Westminster Abbey

Fig 64   The Strand

By the fourteenth century, London had become the capital of England. This brought wealth, power and influence and as a result it became a centre for fashion, society, and entertainment. It retains these functions today (Fig 65).

In the seventeenth and eighteenth centuries London developed as a major port. It had the right physical requirements: a deep, easy to dredge channel; and river banks made of soft clay which made it easy to build docks. Also, it was well situated for trade with the continent. The growth in trade encouraged the banking and insurance industries (Fig 66) which, in turn, provided financial backing for trade and shipping.

In the nineteenth century the **Industrial Revolution** and the wide range of imports encouraged the growth of manufacturing industry. Migrants from all over the country came in search of work and London's population went up faster than ever before (Fig 67). As its population increased, the demand for services such as shops and transport grew and this attracted even more people to London.

Transport developments made London the hub of the nation's transport network (Fig 68) and led to the growth of suburbs (Fig 69). London spread outwards (a process known as sprawl) at a faster and faster rate, often following the main roads and railways (Fig 70). It swallowed up villages and towns; farm land was built on; and in 1945 it seemed possible that London might join up with Birmingham to form a megalopolis. In order to stop this from happening London was given a **Green Belt** (a ring of land around a settlement on which almost all new building is banned); this is explained in more detail in Section 2.7.

Fig 65   West End entertainments

Fig 66   The City

Year	Population (millions)
1801	1.0
1851	2.5
1901	6.0
1951	8.5
1961	8.0
1971	7.5
1981	6.7
1991	6.4

Fig 67   Population change in London

Fig 68   Paddington Station

Fig 69 Suburbs: Catford, South London

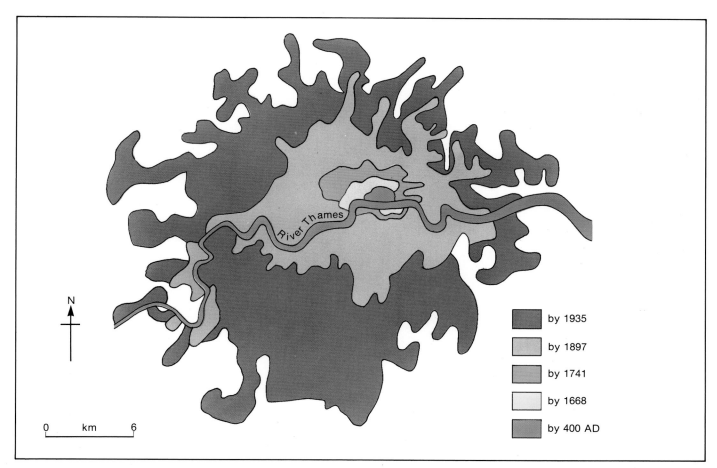

River Thames

N

0 km 6

	by 1935
	by 1897
	by 1741
	by 1668
	by 400 AD

Fig 70 The growth of London

At the end of the Second World War the central areas of London were in urgent need of repair. There had been considerable bomb damage and large areas of Victorian housing in the inner city were in a very poor condition. This period saw the beginning of a movement of people out of the inner city to the overspill estates and New Towns that were built in the post-war years (see Section 2.7).

This trend is still going on, but althouth there are depressed areas in the inner city, London is still the UK's major conurbation. It is still the centre of government; a world centre for banking and insurance; a major manufacturing city; a major port (although most of this activity has moved downstream to Tilbury Docks); it has a thriving tourist industry; it is the leading centre for entertainments; and the development of Heathrow, Gatwick and Stanstead airports has made London an international, as well as a national, route centre.

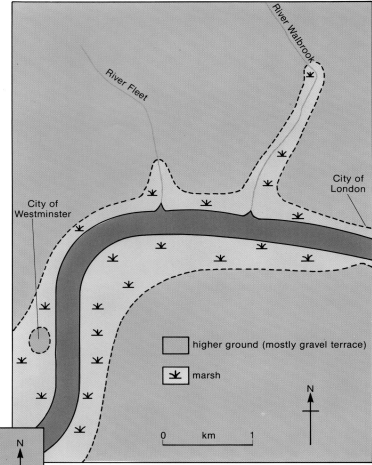

Fig 71   The site of London

Fig 72   London: situation and routeways

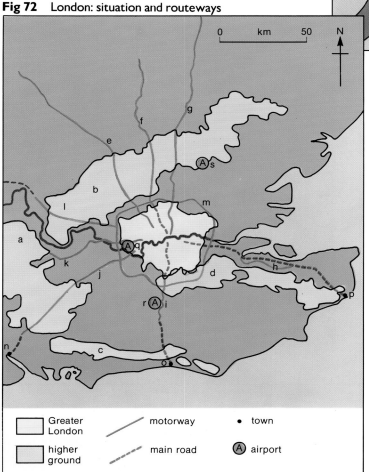

1   Make a copy of Fig 71. Describe the site of London. Explain why you think the Romans chose the present day City of London as the site for their settlement.

2   Make a copy of Fig 72. Using an atlas, label the names of the higher ground (a-d), motorways (e-m), towns (n-p), and airports (q-s). Describe London's situation. What do you think the advantages of London's situation are?

3   Write an account of London's growth and development under the following headings:

   A)   physical factors;
   B)   economic factors;
   C)   political and social factors.

4   Before the nineteenth century did London expand more to the north or to the south of the Thames? What happened during the nineteenth century?

5   What do you notice about the amount of land added to London's built-up area between 1741 and 1897 compared with the amount added between 1897 and 1935?

6   What does the 'finger-like' pattern to London's boundary in 1935 tell us about the way in which London had been growing?

7   What was the maximum straight line distance across London in **a)** 1668 and **b)** 1935?

8   Why do you think swallowing up farm land could be a problem?

2.4 What are towns and cities like, and why?

Land use zones in Huntingdon

Huntingdon is a small town in Cambridgeshire with a population of 15 000. It has many things in common with other small towns; for example, the main shops, offices and banks are found in the town centre and there are modern housing estates on its outskirts. Its main land use zones are shown in Fig 73.

Fig 73 Huntingdon's land use zones

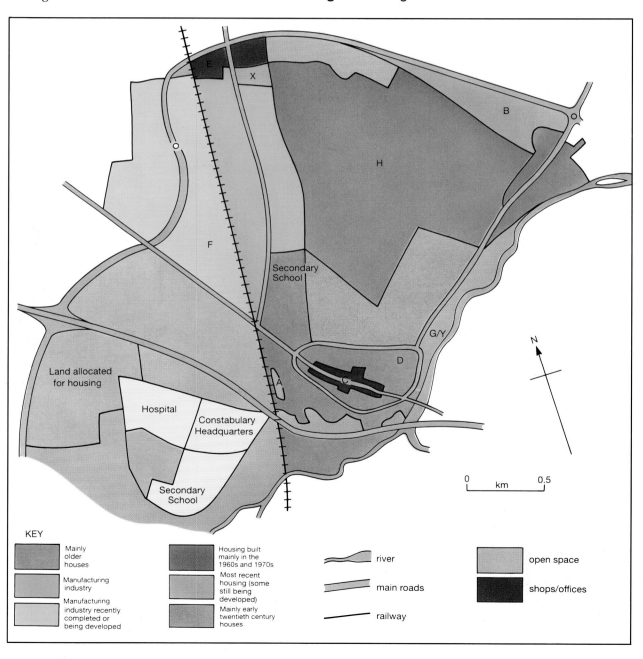

KEY

Mainly older houses	Housing built mainly in the 1960s and 1970s	river
Manufacturing industry	Most recent housing (some still being developed)	main roads
Manufacturing industry recently completed or being developed	Mainly early twentieth century houses	railway
		open space
		shops/offices

Land allocated for housing

Hospital

Constabulary Headquarters

Secondary School

Secondary School

A

B

C

D

E

F

G/Y

H

Fig 73 continued

1   Match the letters on Fig 73 with the following descriptions:
Central Business District (CBD) – the main area of shops, offices and banks: the town centre, or High Street;
Old Industrial Areas – places where there have been industries for many years;
New Light Industrial Estates – places where industries have been set up in recent years. They use light, easy to transport raw materials and produce light, easy to transport finished goods; e.g. plastics and electronics;
Older Housing Areas – zones of housing dating from Edwardian, Victorian and earlier times;
Modern Housing Estates – residential areas built in recent years;
Newer Housing Areas – zones of housing built mainly between the 1920s and the 1970s;
Recreation Areas – parks, playing fields or open space where people relax or take part in leisure activities;
Out-of-town Shopping Centre – a new superstore on the outskirts of the town.
2   Why do you think the main area of shops, offices and banks is in the CBD?
3   Why is Hungtindon's CBD no longer in the centre of the town?

4   Why do you think a new superstore has been built on the outskirts of the town, rather than in the town centre?
5   Why do you think there are only a few factories left in the Old Industrial Areas?
6   Why do you think the New Light Industrial Estates are on the outskirts of the town?
7   Why do you think that **a)** there is a sports ground at place X and **b)** there is a park and play area at place Y on Fig 73?
8   What has made it difficult for Huntingdon to grow **a)** westwards and **b)** south-eastwards?
9   Look at the pie graph in Fig 74. What types of land use other than shops, offices and banks are found in the typical CBD? For each of these types of land use explain why you think they are found in the CBD.
10   Look at Fig 75. What do you notice about the height and spacing of the buildings compared with other parts of the town? Why do you think this is so? Why do you think that the shops are at street level but that the flats and offices are on the first floor?

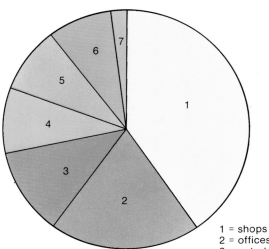

Fig 74   Land use in a typical CBD

1 = shops
2 = offices, including banks
3 = entertainments, such as cinemas, restaurants, museums
4 = open space, such as parks
5 = residential land-use
6 = car parks and taxi ranks
7 = bus station

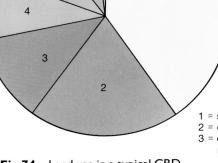

Fig 75   Huntingdon's CBD

The growth and development of Calcutta

Calcutta is India's second largest city, after Bombay, with a population of over ten million. It has been built on the Ganges **delta** next to the Hooghly River. The land use zones of the main part of the city are shown in Fig 76 but the conurbation as a whole extends some 65 km to the north.

Its site has presented many problems because it is liable to flood. However, its situation has given it many advantages: it is a bridging point; the river is navigable to ocean going vessels; it has a rich agricultural and industrial **hinterland** (the Damodar Valley, one of the country's main industrial regions is only 150 miles to the north west); and it is far enough from the sea to be protected from the worst effects of the cyclones which sweep up the Bay of Bengal.

Calcutta was founded by the British in 1690 as a port town for exporting agricultural produce to Britain. It also served as an administration centre and as a garrison (a place where troops are based) and this explains why the port zone, business district and Fort William are found close together.

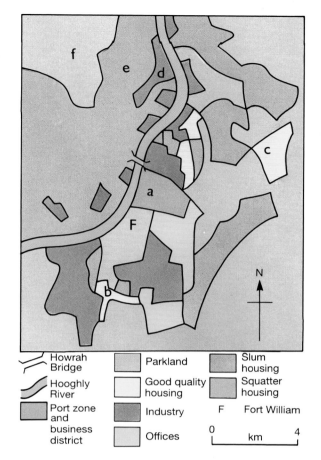

Howrah Bridge	Parkland	Slum housing
Hooghly River	Good quality housing	Squatter housing
Port zone and business district	Industry	F Fort William
	Offices	0 ___ km ___ 4

Fig 76 Land use zones: Calcutta

Fig 77 The High Court

The European sector of the city was built close to the business district and was separated from the native sector by open ground. It had large houses and wide streets. The better quality housing still tends to be near the business district (Fig 78), or near parkland, or away from the city altogether in the suburbs.

Manufacturing industry has grown up mainly next to the river. Jute milling was introduced in the 1850s (jute is a plant which can be used to make sacking, mats and rope). Local coal and iron ore allowed the development of an iron and steel industry and Calcutta is now a centre for textiles, chemicals, metals, engineering and shipbuilding (Fig 79).

Native housing grew up next to these industrial areas. Much of it consisted of tenements – blocks of flats four or five storeys high – of a similar design to those built in Britain's towns and cities in the nineteenth century. Many of these tenements are still standing but they are in a very poor condition (Fig 80).

Fig 78 Calcutta Mansions, Chittaranjan Avenue

Fig 79 Weaving cotton goods

Fig 80 Central Calcutta

In recent years, Calcutta's population has increased dramatically (Fig 81) mainly because of rural-urban migration. The shortage of housing has led to the growth of **squatter settlements**, called 'bustees' (Fig 82). Also, it is estimated that more than 100 000 people have no home at all and sleep on the streets.

The bustees tend to be built on disused land near the city centre where it is easy to pick up casual work (e.g. selling fruit, carrying bags, or shining shoes); on undeveloped land next to 'dirty' industries; and on the outskirts of the city where land is available. They are usually illegal and conditions are extremely poor with as many as 25 people sharing a tap and a toilet (see Section 2.8).

Urban models

Towns and cities have many things in common. For example, there is usually a business district in the town centre where the main shops, offices and banks are found, and housing on the outskirts. These similarities have led geographers to develop models – plans of what you would expect a city to be like in theory – to help our understanding of real towns and cities.

ENQUIRY

1   Use an atlas to help you draw and label a sketch map to show the advantages and disadvantages of Calcutta's site and situation.
2   Which factors have been of particular importance to Calcutta's growth and development?
3   For each of the land use zones marked with a letter on Fig 76, describe and explain its location.
4   What differences are there between the location and appearance of the main housing areas in Calcutta and the housing areas in Huntingdon (see Fig 73, page 48)?

Fig 81   Population growth: Calcutta

Fig 82   Bustee

One of the most straightforward theories is the *concentric model* (Fig 83). Its form is explained by five main processes:

- **Accessibility.** The business district is in the centre because it is the easiest place in the town for everyone to get to, wherever they live.
- **Concentric growth.** Towns grow outwards from a central point, like ripples on a pond.
- **Concentric decay.** Each zone gets older at the same rate.
- **Attraction.** Some types of land use try to be near each other; e.g. firms which provide services for the CBD, such as office supplies, will want to be near their customers so they will choose a location on the edge of the town centre.
- **Repulsion.** Some types of land use try to avoid each other; for example, the occupants of upper class residential areas do not want to be near industry and, because they can afford to separate home and work, they choose a location in the suburbs.

However, the concentric model ignores transport routes which are a very important influence on the form of towns and cities. This has led to the development of another theory, known as the *sector model* (Fig 84).

In this model, sector growth replaces concentric growth as the most important process with different types of land use developing alongside main roads, railways and rivers. The processes of accessibility, attraction and repulsion still operate, so the business district is found in the centre of the town; service industries locate near their customers; and upper class housing is located away from industry. Concentric decay also affects this pattern.

CBD (Central Business District) This is the main area of shops, offices and entertainments.

Inner city This is also known as the 'transition zone' or 'twilight zone'. It is a mixture of run down buildings at or near the end of their lives; areas of redevelopment and renewal; and traditional manufacturing industries, many of which are in decline. It often has a high percentage of immigrants and its communities are usually poor.

Inner suburbs These were the first suburbs to be built and their age means that they are often in need of repair. Communities are usually more settled and better off than in the inner city.

Outer suburbs The best housing is usually found here. This zone is furthest away from the city centre and is the area of most recent growth.

Urban-rural fringe Traditionally, this has been a mixture of farmland, open space and dormitory settlement. However, in recent years it has seen a great deal of development because new light industries and out-of-town shopping centres have been attracted by good road transport.

Fig 83   Concentric model of urban structure

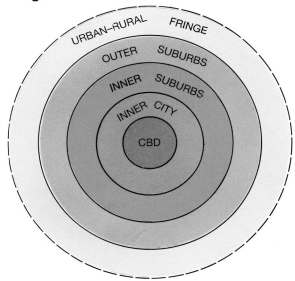

Fig 84   Sector model of urban structure

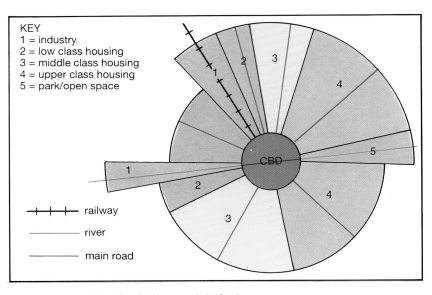

KEY
1 = industry
2 = low class housing
3 = middle class housing
4 = upper class housing
5 = park/open space

railway

river

main road

Neither of these models is designed to explain the form of conurbations – large towns or cities which are the result of smaller settlements merging together. These have more than one 'centre': London (see Section 2.3) is a good example. This has led to the development of the *multiple nuclei model* (Fig 85) which combines ideas from both the concentric and sector models but allows a city to have several growth points, or nuclei.

All three of these models ignore important factors which affect the form of a town or city. Relief can have a major influence; for example, high ground often attracts upper class residential development whereas low class housing is forced to occupy less favourable sites, such as low ground which is liable to flood – compare Hampstead and Kilburn in London. Rivers can be a barrier to development. The 'vertical' dimension is important: land use patterns change as you go up a building (see Fig 75) which helps to explain why luxury flats can be found in the CBD. The town centre is no longer necessarily the easiest place to get to because of the increase in road traffic, hence the growth of industry and shops on the outskirts of towns and cities. Planning decisions, such as inner city redevelopment schemes, also have a big effect on the form of the city.

Also, towns and cities in LEDCs do not necessarily follow the same pattern as those in MEDCs and this has led to the development of models such as the model of an Asian city (Fig 86). This model emphasises a number of points:

- many Asian cities began as ports in colonial times;
- European and native sectors were originally separated;
- growth has been inland away from the port;
- high class residential areas have remained near the CBD because this is where their occupants work, and where the best entertainments and facilities are found;
- squatter settlements have grown up on the edge of the city because this is where most vacant land is to be found.

A model is only of use if it helps us to explain what exists: the following Enquiry (page 56) allows you to evaluate the models described in this section.

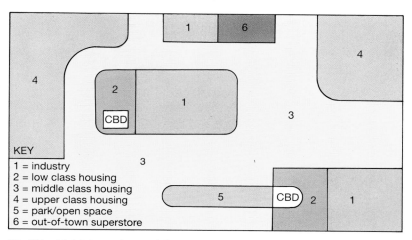

Fig 85   Multiple nuclei model

KEY
1 = industry
2 = low class housing
3 = middle class housing
4 = upper class housing
5 = park/open space
6 = out-of-town superstore

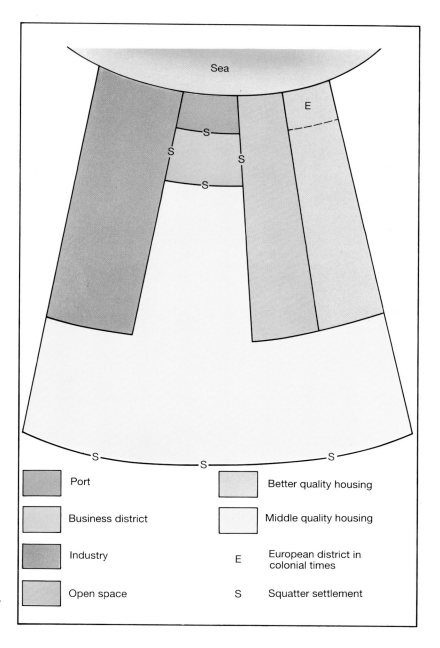

Fig 86   A model of the structure of an Asian city

Port

Business district

Industry

Open space

Better quality housing

Middle quality housing

E   European district in colonial times

S   Squatter settlement

1   For each of the land use zones in the concentric model, explain the main process which accounts for its location.

2   What is the main difference between the sector model and the concentric model? What are the similarities?

3   Why is the multiple nuclei model useful for explaining the form of conurbations?

4   What processes are at work in the model of the Asian City?

5   Compare Huntingdon's land use zones (Fig 73, page 48) with the concentric and sector models. Which of the two models does it most closely resemble? Explain and justify your answer. Are there any ways in which it disagrees with both models?

6   Compare Calcutta's land use zones (Fig 76, page 51) with the model of an Asian city. In what ways does it agree and disagree with the model?

7   Overall, how useful do you think these models are for explaining the form of towns and cities?

2.5 Where do we do our shopping, and why?

When we go shopping we not only have to decide what to buy but we also have to decide where to buy it. There are corner shops selling milk, sweets and newspapers; there are shopping parades with a butchers, a bakers, a greengrocers and a small supermarket; there is the high street; there are shopping malls; and there is the out-of-town superstore (Fig 87). These different types of shop and shopping centres are found in different locations and a number of factors helps to explain their distribution.

Fig 87   Shops and shopping centres

(i)   Corner shop

(ii) Shopping parade

(iv) The entrance to Queensgate Shopping Mall, Peterborough

(iii) High Street

(v) Out-of-town superstore

Range of good

Range of good means how far we are prepared to travel for a particular good/service.

Usually, we are only prepared to travel a short distance for the things we need every day like milk, bread or newspapers. This explains why corner shops and shopping parades which sell these types of goods – known as low order or convenience goods – are found in villages and in the suburbs of towns and cities.

However, we are usually prepared to travel longer distances for the things we need less often like clothes, a carpet or a new radio. This explains why shops which sell these types of goods – known as high order or comparison goods – are only found in the larger shopping centres such as the high street or the shopping mall.

ENQUIRY

1 Read through the five groups of goods/services below. Write out each group putting the good/service you would be prepared to travel the shortest distance for first and the good/service you would be prepared to travel the longest distance for last.
a) weekly groceries; bread; a personal computer;
b) a deep freeze; a bank; sweets;
c) potatoes; the doctors; an antique piece of furniture;
d) wallpaper and paint; a pound of mince; a stereo system;
e) a cassette or compact disc; a can of lemonade; a Premier League football match.

2 Now make three lists. Under the heading '1st (low) order goods/services' write down the items from each group that you said you were prepared to travel the shortest distance for. Do the same for your '2nd' and '3rd' (high) order goods/ services.

3 Compare your lists with those of the rest of the class. They are hopefully very similar!

4 Why do you think 1st (low) order goods/services are known as **convenience goods/services**?

5 Why do you think 3rd (high) order goods/services are known as **comparison goods/services**?

Threshold of entry

Threshold of entry means the size a settlement has to be before it can have a particular type of shop, or offer a particular type of service. Usually, small settlements only have convenience stores – they do not have enough customers to make it worthwhile for a large store to open up. However, large settlements can support shops selling comparison goods because there are so many customers. Convenience goods are also found in large settlements because the people who live there need them.

ENQUIRY

1 Write out the following list of goods/ services in three columns. The first column should be for the ones you would expect to find in a village, the second for the ones you would expect to find in a small town, and the third for the ones you would expect to find in a city.

secondary school	supermarket
greengrocer's	a bank's Head Office
record shop	a big department
theatre	store
newsagent's	butcher's

2 Compare your lists with those of the rest of the class. As in the previous Enquiry your results should be very similar.

3 Now divide the lists up into 1st, 2nd, and 3rd order goods/services. What do you notice about the 'order' of goods/ services offered by the different sizes of settlement?

4 Can you think of, and explain, any exceptions to the threshold of entry rule?

Sphere of influence

By **sphere of influence** we mean the area a settlement serves. The larger the sphere of influence, the more goods/services a settlement can offer. This helps to explain why towns and cities which are in the centre of a region – and therefore accessible (easy to get to) from many other settlements – usually have the biggest range of comparison goods/ services: quite simply, they have the greatest number of possible customers.

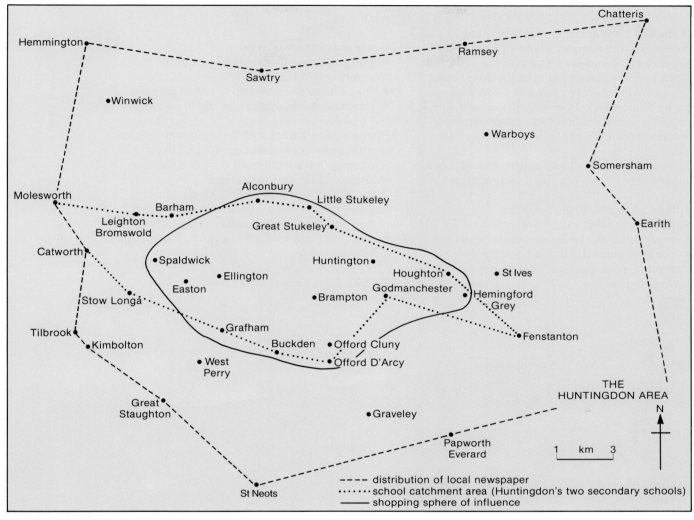

Fig 88 Spheres of influence map

Fig 88 shows the results of a spheres of influence survey carried out by a group of Year Ten pupils in Huntingdon, a small town in Cambridgeshire, which provides mainly 2nd order goods and services. What do you notice about the size and shape of the spheres of influence of the different goods and services offered by Huntingdon? Try to explain the differences you can see.

Out-of-town superstores

In the last 20 years there has been a big increase in the number of out-of-town superstores. Land is cheaper on the edge of a town so firms can afford to build their stores at ground level and to provide large, free car parks. Supermarkets and do-it-yourself shops, in particular, have been attracted to these locations (See Fig 89).

Compared with the town centre, out-of-town superstores have a number of advantages:

- they are easier to get to by car;
- parking is easy;
- everything can be bought under one roof;
- prices are usually lower because superstores can pass on 'bulk purchase' savings to their customers.

However, they have their disadvantages as well:

- not everyone has a car;
- you cannot go from shop to shop comparing goods;
- they add to the problem of urban sprawl;
- they take trade away from the town centre.

Planning applications for new superstores are often bitterly contested (Fig 90) and even when they have been built they can cause a great deal of controversy (Fig 91). However, they are very popular with their customers and very profitable for their owners, and with car ownership still rising they look set to be a permanent feature of the shopping landscape.

Fig 89   Brent Cross, North London

ENQUIRY

1   Why is it an advantage for a superstore to be built at ground level?
2   Why do you think supermarkets and do-it-yourself stores, in particular, are attracted to out-of-town locations?
3   What do you think are **a)** the two main advantages and **b)** the two main disadvantages of out-of-town superstores? Explain your choice.
4   What do you think of the objections being expressed in Figs 90 and 91?

Fig 90 Which superstore for St Neots?

Store giants in town site battle

A STORE war is hotting up as rival retailers compete to win the supermarket battle of St Neots.

Although planning officers looked set to back the Safeway development on the Eynesbury Rovers site, last-minute plans submitted by Tesco threw the decision back into the melting pot.

With both stores offering a tempting package of community benefits, councillors and residents claim the final decision will hinge on which store comes up with the best deal for the people of St Neots.

Safeway has offered £150,000 for traffic calming and £300,000 for town centre improvements as part of its planning proposal.

If the Safeway proposal goes ahead developers Wyncote have also pledged to provide a new purpose-built football ground valued at £1.7m.

Tesco is offering £60,000 for traffic calming and £600,000 for town centre improvements.

The Ramsey Post, 29 July 1993

Fig 91 The town centre protests

TOWN'S SLOW DEATH

CARELESS mis-management by Huntingdon District Council is to blame for the town's high street dying a slow death claims one angry trader.

Thousands of people, including 25 High Street Traders have supported a petition condemning the opening of the new Tesco store, claiming it will result in a ghost town with high parking fees.

On behalf of the traders, owner of Starburger, Hasan Kamil-Hasan has written an open letter to local people claiming the council has put up the parking fees in the town to coincide with Tesco offering free parking.

He said: 'In a way they are telling people to stay away from the High Street.'

The Town Crier, 17 April 1993

Central place theory

A **central place** is a settlement which provides goods and services for the area around it. If we assume that a region is uniform throughout – e.g. no hills, valleys, rivers, deposits of raw materials etc – and that people make rational decisions about where to shop, we can work out what the ideal distribution of central places would be.

Since people prefer to travel short distances for things they need frequently (low order/ convenience goods and services), we would expect to find a relatively large number of small central places. On the other hand, people are prepared to travel further for things they need less often (high order/comparison goods and services), so we would expect to find a relatively small number of large central places.

We can also expect people to travel to the nearest central place. As a result, settlements which provide the same order of goods and services should be the same distance apart: if one settlement was further away than all the others it would get very few customers.

However, if central places are the same distance apart their spheres of influence – which are circular – must overlap. This means that people who live half way between two central places do not know which one to go to. We can assume, therefore, that in an ideal world each settlement has an hexagonal sphere of influence in order to get round this problem.

The following Enquiry (page 62) will help you to understand these ideas more fully.

1   Make a large copy of Fig 92. Study the key carefully so that you understand what is being shown.

2   Each 1st order settlement has reached the threshold of entry required for supplying 1st order goods and services. The radius of the sphere of influence of each of these settlements is 1 km. Using a compass, draw on each 1st order settlement its sphere of influence. (Do this for settlements which are 2nd order as well as 1st order.)

3   You will notice that the spheres of influence overlap. In order to avoid this draw a line along the middle of each overlap to produce a series of hexagons.

4   Each 2nd order settlement not only supplies 1st order goods and services but it has also reached the threshold of entry required for supplying 2nd order goods and services. The sphere of influence of these settlements reaches out to the six nearest 1st order settlements. Draw on these spheres of influence. Avoid overlaps by making them hexagonal.

5   Compare the number of 1st order and 2nd order settlements.

6   Comment on the spacing of the 1st and 2nd order settlements.

7   What do you notice about the shape and size of each sphere of influence?

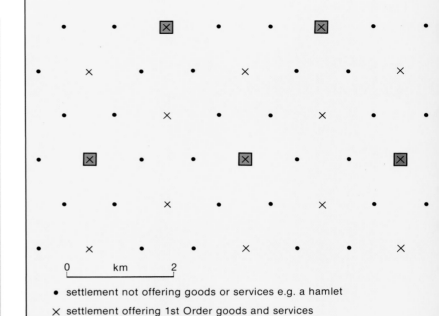

Fig 92   Central places

A theory is only of use if it helps us to explain what really exists. Central place theory requires us to assume a uniform landscape and sensible behaviour – both of which are rarely, if ever, true! If it is close to what really exists, though, it could still be use.

The following Enquiry allows you to test out the main ideas of the theory, namely:
– there are more low order than high order settlements;
– settlements of the same order are the same distance apart;
– spheres of influence are hexagonal.

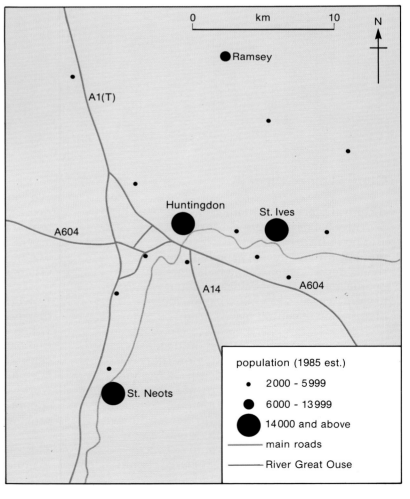

Fig 93   Settlement distribution in the Huntingdon area

ENQUIRY

1 Study Fig 93. Which of the main ideas of central place theory does the distribution of settlements on this map agree with? In what ways does the distribution disagree with the theory? Can you explain any of the differences?

2 Think about the assumptions we had to make for central place theory to work and then try to explain why the perfect world predicted by the theory does not exist in reality. Here are some ideas to help you:

- commuters often do not get home until the shops in their settlement have closed;

- central places offering the same order of goods and services as each other can have different stores e.g. some might have a John Lewis while others might have a Debenhams;

- if there is a good road or rail link a central place which is further away in distance can be quicker to get to in time;

- it could be that your best friend lives in a central place which is further away than the one you would be expected to go to.

2.6 Assessment task: *Shopping patterns and central place theory*

Aims

This survey allows you to test a number of ideas about:

- range of good;
- threshold of entry;
- spheres of influence;
- central place theory.

Method

- Choose a study area of not more than 400 square kilometres.
- Find out the population of the settlements in your study area from the local library.
- Compare **either** three settlements – for example, a village, a small town and a large town or city – **or** three shopping centres – for example, a corner shop, a neighbourhood shopping parade and the town centre.
- Draw up a questionnaire like the one in Fig 94. Interview 30 people in each place.

- Your school will have information about catchment areas (where pupils come from). Use this to find out the spheres of influence of local primary and secondary schools.
- The free newspapers that come through the door make most of their money from advertising. They always give their distribution area – the area the papers are sent to – which is their 'advertising' sphere of influence.

Writing up your results

- State the aims of the survey.
- Explain how you carried out the survey.

Fig 94 Sphere of influence record table

SHOPPING SURVEY RECORD TABLE												

Location _____   Date _____

Number of shops selling 1st Order goods and services_____

2nd Order _____   3rd Order _____

QUESTION / PERSON	Where do you live?	How did you get here?					What are you buying?			How often do you visit these shops?			
		car	bus	bike	walk	other	convenience goods	comparison goods	both	less often	once a month	once a week	more often
1													
2													

Presentation of results

• Draw a sketch map of your study area. Mark on the location of each settlement with a coloured dot according to its place in the settlement hierarchy (see Fig 43, page 32).
• Count up the number of shops selling 1st order, 2nd order and 3rd order goods/services in each of your three study locations and draw bar charts to show the results.
• Draw onto the base map a line from each shopper's home to the place where you did the survey. Use different coloured lines to show how they get to the shops e.g. blue for car, red for bike. Join up the furthest points to show the size and shape of the sphere of influence.
• Draw a bar chart to show how often the shoppers visit the survey area.
• Draw onto the base map the spheres of influence of local primary and secondary schools.
• Draw onto the base map the 'advertising' spheres of influence of the free newspapers.

Interpretation and explanation

• For each of the three places you studied in detail, describe and explain their location.

• Did people use different methods of transport to get to the different locations? If they did, try to explain why.
• What do your results tell you about the following ideas?
    – people travel further for some goods than others;
    – the larger the settlement (or shopping centre) the greater the number of shops selling comparison (high order) goods;
    – the larger the settlement (or shopping centre) the larger the sphere of influence;
    – different goods/services have different spheres of influence.
• To what extent do your map, and the results of your survey, agree with the main ideas of central place theory (see page 61)?

Conclusions and limitations

• Summarise your main findings.
• Did you have any problems carrying out the survey? If you were to do it again are there any ways in which you would try to improve it?

2.7 Change in the city – why does it happen and how do we manage it?

Towns and cities the world over are always changing. For example, new housing estates are built; areas become run down; and populations rise and fall. Some of the main processes of change are examined below.

Suburbanisation

When towns and cities in Europe and North America began to grow rapidly in the first half of the nineteenth century, the main means of transport were foot and horse. This meant that all classes of people, rich and poor, had to live fairly close to where they worked.

However, the development of transport – first trains, then trams, buses and cars – meant that those who could afford to do so could separate home and work and commute in to the CBD from quieter, pleasanter housing areas on the outskirts of the town, known as suburbs.

The growth of these suburbs – the process of **suburbanisation** (Fig 95) – has brought with it

advantages and disadvantages. Land gets cheaper as you move away from the centre of a town, so houses and gardens can be bigger. There is less industry, less traffic and more open space. However, the journey to work can often be long, tiring and uncomfortable and it bring with it the problems of the rush hour and traffic congestion in the CBD (Fig 96).

The suburbs of a town or city are far from being one continuous type of housing. For example, in London the housing quality of the suburbs nearer to the city centre (Fig 97) tends to be lower than that of the suburbs further away from the city centre (Fig 98). This is because the inner suburbs were built first and are in the greatest need of repair. What tends to happen is that as the inner suburbs become run down those who can afford to do so move even further out of the city, while less well-off people replace them. This process is known as **social leap-frogging** and is repeated as the suburbs grow.

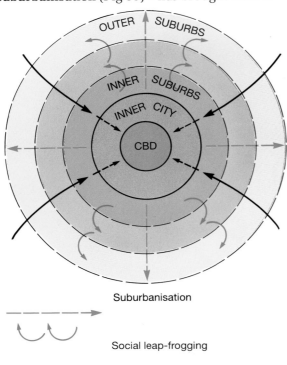

Suburbanisation

Social leap-frogging

Gentrification

Fig 95 Suburbanisation, social leap-frogging and gentrification

Fig 96 Traffic congestion during the rush hour

Fig 97   Inner suburbs: Islington, London

Fig 98   Outer suburbs: Hampstead, London

Gentrification

Another process which is changing the character of residential areas in many large towns and cities is **gentrification**. This happens when wealthy people move into a run-down area. Property is bought at a low price, is renovated and then goes up in value. Until the process is finished you can have very expensive houses next to run-down houses.

Gentrification is happening in large areas of London's inner suburbs e.g. Islington and Fulham. Fig 99 shows an interesting example of 'going up-market' with a luxury development in a disused dockland warehouse.

Fig 99   A dockland warehouse development

1 Draw and label simple diagrams to explain what is meant by the processes of suburbanisation, social leap-frogging and gentrification.

2 Why do most people prefer to live away from where they work? Why are certain groups of people unable to move to the suburbs? What could be the advantages of more people living closer to where they work?

3 What effects – good and bad – does gentrification have on the people and environment of an area? Consider the existing population and the people moving in.

4 Study Fig 100 which shows the growth of the London Underground between 1863 and 1986. It is a topological map, which means that distances and directions are not true. Why do you think the map has been drawn like this? Compare it with a map of London (e.g. in a road atlas) and give two examples of misleading distances between stations and two examples of misleading directions between stations. Now compare it with Fig 70, page 45. Can you identify any relationships between the growth of London and the development of the Underground system?

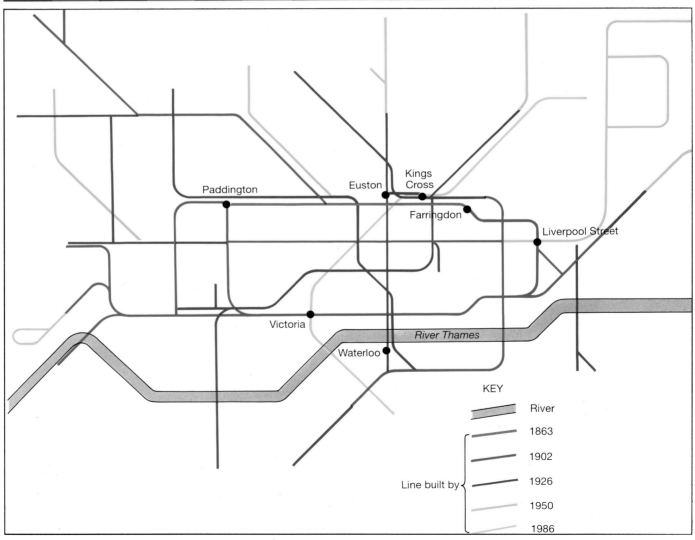

Fig 100   The growth of the London Underground 1863–1986

Inner City redevelopment

The **inner city** is the zone which surrounds the CBD. In most towns in the UK it grew up in the nineteenth century and by the 1950s much of it was in need of repair (Fig 101). It is also known as the transition zone, or twilight zone, because it is an area of change where buildings at the end of their lives are demolished or put to other uses.

Housing is one of the main problems in inner city areas. For example, by 1945 in London's inner city many houses were over 75 years old and in urgent need of repair: war time bombing had made things worse (Fig 102). One way in which the planners tried to tackle this problem was to encourage many thousands of people to move to New Towns and Overspill Estates (see Section 2.7). Another way was to bulldoze the slum districts completely and to build new housing, a policy known as **comprehensive redevelopment**.

The run-down buildings were mainly replaced with deck-access housing (Fig 103) or high-rise flats (Fig 104). However, these new types of buildings brought with them their own problems.

Fig 101   Inner city decay: Hackney, London

Fig 102   Bomb damage to the inner city

Fig 103   Deck-access housing, Sheffield

Fig 104   High-rise flats: Hulme, Manchester

Deck-access housing gave very little privacy because people had to walk past their neighbours' front doors and windows. This helps to explain the high crime rate associated with these developments.

The high-rise flats presented particular problems for parents with young families and for elderly people, especially as the lifts often broke down. You could not keep an eye on the entrances, corridors and stairs and this made them unsafe. There were problems with damp and condensation and many of them developed cracks and became unsafe only a few years after they had been put up. In 1968 a gas explosion caused one whole section of a block of flats to collapse at Ronan Point in Canning Town.

Problems like these led to a change of policy and in the early 1970s comprehensive redevelopment was replaced by the idea of **urban renewal**. The main aim was to renovate, which means to 'do up' or modernise old buildings, instead of knocking them down. Grants were given for repairs and for putting in indoor toilets and bathrooms. Local communities were involved in decisions about how their areas should be improved. However, the scale of the problem was so great that the inner city still stood out as a problem area in the 1980s (Fig 105).

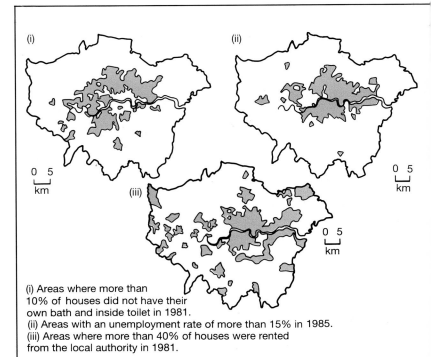

(i) Areas where more than 10% of houses did not have their own bath and inside toilet in 1981.
(ii) Areas with an unemployment rate of more than 15% in 1985.
(iii) Areas where more than 40% of houses were rented from the local authority in 1981.

Fig 105   Housing deprivation in London 1981

More recently, developments of the 1950s and 1960s have been demolished and are being replaced with low-rise housing built according to the nineteenth century street layout (Fig 106).

After 20 years, these are coming down
. . . and it's back to square one
with terraced houses

ONE of the most notorious estates in London is to be pulled down and replaced by small terrace houses similar to those demolished in the 1970s to make way for flats.

Labour-controlled Hackney Borough Council announced yesterday that it would pull down the Holly Street Estate. Over the next five years, the 16 system-built five-storey blocks will be replaced by Laing-built homes in the £64 million scheme. It will follow the street layout of late Victorian days. Four 19-storey tower blocks and three smaller ones will also go.

The flats suffer from poor insulation, leaks and condensation, defective heating and inadequate fire separation. They are infested with cockroaches, ants, rats and mice. Mr John McCafferty, council leader, said 100 per cent council ownership would be replaced by a mixture of private houses, housing association homes and accommodation for the elderly.

The council's successful City Challenge entry, the Department of the Environment, the Housing Corporation and developers will provide the money.

The Daily Telegraph, 12 December 1992

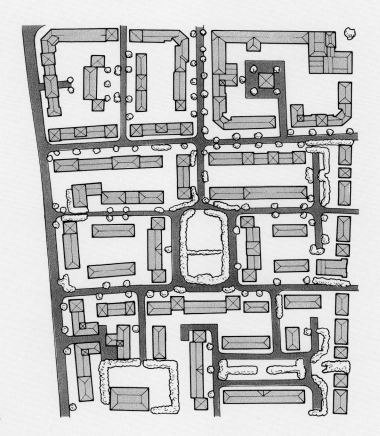

Fig 106   Redeveloping the Holly Street Estate, Hackney

Fig 107   The inner city housing problem

```
┌──────────────┐     ┌──────────────┐     ┌──────────────┐
│  Inner city  │ ──▶ │              │ ──▶ │              │
└──────────────┘     └──────────────┘     └──────────────┘
        ▲                                          │
        │                                          ▼
┌──────────────┐     ┌──────────────┐     ┌──────────────┐
│              │ ◀── │              │ ◀── │              │
└──────────────┘     └──────────────┘     └──────────────┘
```

ENQUIRY

1 Copy Fig 107 and complete it by adding the following labels in their correct box. What does this diagram tell you about the cause of housing problems in the inner city?
   a) low incomes mean less money for repair and maintenance;
   b) built in the nineteenth century;
   c) poorer people can afford to live here because run-down housing is cheaper;
   d) in need of repair;
   e) houses become more run-down.

2 What were the problems with deck-access housing and multi-storey flats? Can you think of any advantages of these types of housing?

3 Explain what is meant by urban renewal. What do you think were the advantages and disadvantages of this policy?

4 What is your opinion of the scheme described in Fig 106?

De-urbanisation

Another change which has affected towns and cities in the UK in recent years is a fall in population. Overall, the percentage of the UK's population living in urban areas has declined from 75 per cent in 1971 to 73.5 per cent in 1991. The rate of decline has been greatest in the main conurbations (see Fig 44, page 33).

Some of the reasons for this process – known as **de-urbanisation** – are given in Figs 108 and

Back to the land trend growing, planners told

By John Ardill,
Environment Correspondent

One in ten of Britain's city dwellers — some 5 million people — will move to the country during the next 30 to 40 years, swelling the population of small towns and villages by half, planners have been told.

The trend is established and will continue whatever governments and local authorities decide to do about it, Mr Henry Clark, head of information for the Council for Small Industries in Rural Areas (CoSira) told the town and country planning summer school in Nottingham. The Environment Secretary, Mr Nicholas Ridley will address it today.

Mr Clark's predictions go to the heart of the hottest issues in British land-use planning: the location of new housing, industrial and commercial development and the emerging plight of a countryside stricken by agricultural decline for the first time in more than half a century.

Planning authorities, fearful of electoral pressure from conservation groups, are trying to restrict development to urban areas, backed officially, but some feel ambivalently, by the Government.

But more and more planners and organisations, aware of the problems and potential of agricultural change, are beginning to challenge this.

Nicholas Ridley:
to address planners

They will be joined in Nottingham today by Mr Jonathon Porritt, director of Friends of the Earth, who will argue for a rural resettlement programme and moves to bring rural occupation into the cities.

Mr Clark, who favours the gradual expansion of towns and villages rather than a new garden city programme, told the school that the 1981 census showed signs of an end to the long decline of the rural population; the 1991 one might show an upward swing, perhaps from 10 million to 10.5 million.

The trend was already clear in Wiltshire, Oxfordshire and perhaps Cambridgeshire, and would extend to other shires although the populations of more peripheral counties were likely to remain stable.

Fig 108   Back to the land

109. It affects both the towns and cities that people are leaving and the rural areas they are moving to. For example, as with most types of migration it tends to be the younger and more active members of a community who leave while older and less ambitious people stay behind. On the other hand, the rural areas have seen village populations rise dramatically; the building of new housing estates; and the growth of new industries (Fig 110).

ENQUIRY

1   Read through Figs 108 and 109. Over the next 30 to 40 years how many people are likely to move 'back to the land'? Give three reasons why more people are choosing to live in the countryside.
2   In what ways do you think this trend will change urban areas? (Think about factors like the character of the community, services such as shops and schools and the general appearance of the area.)
3   In what ways do you think this trend will change rural areas? (Think about factors like village life, services and employment opportunities.)

Increased separation of home and workplace has been a continuing trend for many decades, brought out by the combination of a changing distribution of employment and easier travel. Decline of agricultural employment and increasing concentration of other types of work in urban centres has led to an increase in commuting from rural to urban areas. The greater growth of jobs, especially in the service sector, in large centres has also led to an increase in commuting from smaller to larger towns.

Coupled with shortage or high costs of housing in and near the larger towns, and the desire for a rural living environment, these trends have led to the development of dormitory housing in progressively wider hinterlands. The ease of travel by private car and the greater choice it provides has led to a general rise in the numbers of journeys to work, irrespective of changes in the availability of local employment. As a result of these trends the overlap between employment catchment areas is becoming much greater and the pattern of movement more complex.

Fig 109   An extract from the Huntingdon Area District Plan, Preliminary Report 1980

Fig 110   A rural industrial estate in Cambridgeshire

Urban planning at the national scale

In the 1920s and 1930s problems such as urban sprawl (60 000 acres of agricultural land were being lost a year) and inner city decay were becoming very serious in many parts of the UK. A number of Commissions of Enquiry were set up and their reports contained a great range of possible solutions. Almost as soon as the war had finished in 1945 many of these ideas were tried out, some with more success than others.

Green Belts

A Green Belt is a ring of land around a settlement on which almost all new building is banned. It therefore stops urban sprawl and as a result, saves farm land and land for recreation and leisure.

A special Act of Parliament allowed London to set up the first Green Belt in 1938. The Town and Country Planning Act of 1947 made it much easier to set them up because it nationalised the right to develop land – this meant that no new building could take place without the permission of the local authority, or the government. By the mid-1950s the government was encouraging all local authorities to use their powers to set up Green Belts around their major towns and cities; the result can be seen in (Fig 111).

Green Belts have been very successful at stopping urban sprawl; for example, less than ten per cent of London's Green Belt has been built on, and the land which has been lost has been for major projects such as motorway construction (Fig 119). However, they have created a number of problems: for example, developers have 'jumped' the Green Belt and built dormitory settlements beyond it, which means long journeys for many commuters; and house prices inside the Green Belts have been forced up because of the demand for land.

Fig 111 The edge of London's Green Belt

Look at Fig 112.

1 Name three conurbations and three towns or cities which have Green Belts around them.

2 In the 1950s commuting into the big conurbations from outside the Green Belts was almost impossible. Why is this no longer the case and what effect could commuting have on the towns and villages just outside the Green Belt? (Think about factors such as population, services, the community, and the environment.)

3 The Green Belt has always been under pressure from developers. Why do developers want to build on the Green Belt? What arguments are there against building on the Green Belt?

(An interesting way to answer this question would be to organise a class Planning Enquiry. Two people should represent a firm of developers who want to build a small industrial estate producing computers and advanced electronic equipment on a 100 acre Green Belt site. They also wish to build houses for the employees, shops and a leisure complex. Two people should represent 'Friends of the Green Belt' and oppose the scheme. One of you will have to be the farmer who owns the land the developers wish to build on. You will also need to elect a Chairperson who will carry out the Enquiry in such a way that everyone has a chance to give their point of view. Those of you who do not have a special job are the 'public'. You can ask questions and at the end of the debate you decide with a show of hands whether or not the development should go ahead. You should then produce a report on the Enquiry.)

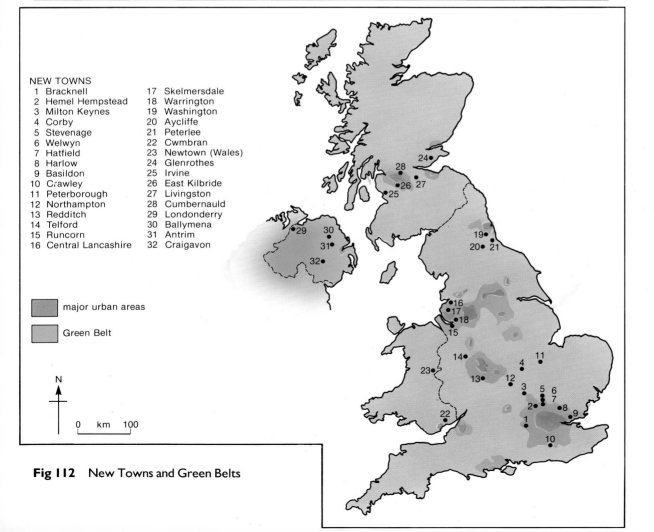

NEW TOWNS

1	Bracknell	17	Skelmersdale
2	Hemel Hempstead	18	Warrington
3	Milton Keynes	19	Washington
4	Corby	20	Aycliffe
5	Stevenage	21	Peterlee
6	Welwyn	22	Cwmbran
7	Hatfield	23	Newtown (Wales)
8	Harlow	24	Glenrothes
9	Basildon	25	Irvine
10	Crawley	26	East Kilbride
11	Peterborough	27	Livingston
12	Northampton	28	Cumbernauld
13	Redditch	29	Londonderry
14	Telford	30	Ballymena
15	Runcorn	31	Antrim
16	Central Lancashire	32	Craigavon

major urban areas

Green Belt

N

0   km   100

Fig 112   New Towns and Green Belts

New Towns and overspill estates

As well as stopping urban sprawl there was also the need to help the over-crowded, run-down areas of our large towns and cities. As one part of the overall solution, it was decided to build two types of new settlement beyond the Green Belt:

- **New Towns.** 32 New Towns have been built (Figs 112 and 113). The first New Towns were planned virtually from scratch, although there was usually a small settlement there to begin with. Since the 1960s a number of New Towns, such as Peterborough, have been built onto existing towns.
- **Overspill Estates.** Areas of housing and industry added on to existing towns e.g. the Oxmoor Estate in Huntingdon (see Fig 73, page 48).

Bracknell	49 024
Hemel Hempstead	76 954
Milton Keynes	96 546
Peterborough	115 544
Northampton	157 217
Corby	47 623
Stevenage	74 507
Welwyn	40 727
Hatfield	25 150
Harlow	79 523
Basildon	94 791
Crawley	72 684
Redditch	63 693
Telford	103 646
Runcorn	64 412
Warrington	135 946
Central Lancashire	247 870
Skelmersdale	39 400
Washington	49 986
Aycliffe	24 518
Peterlee	22 919
Cwmbran	44 316
Newtown	8 651
*Glenrothes	38 650
*Irvine	55 495
*East Kilbride	69 453
*Livingston	40 631
*Cumbernauld	49 781
Londonderry	90 000
Ballymena	50 000
Antrim	30 000
Craigavon	70 000

Fig 113   The population of the UK's New Towns 1981 (*1991)

1	to be self-contained; 80% of working population to be employed within the town itself
2	to have medium to low density housing
3	to have an informal road pattern
4	residential areas to be organised into neighbourhood units each with its own schools, shops etc
5	industrial areas to be separated from residential areas but to still be within walking or biking distance
6	to have planned parks and open spaces
7	to have an easy-to-get-to CBD, the main shopping area to be pedestrianised i.e. traffic-free

Fig 114   New Towns, main aims and objectives

Stevenage New Town

Stevenage was the first New Town to be approved, in 1946. Before the 'New Town' was built 'Old Stevenage' had a population of only 6000. In 1981 it had a population of 75 000.

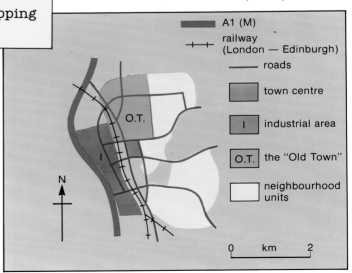

Fig 115   Stevenage: town plan

New Towns have not been entirely successful. They have been criticised for being unfriendly, ugly, and boring. The aim of being self-contained has been difficult to achieve – for example, an increasing number of people commute to London from New Towns such as Basildon and Stevenage. Roads in many of the early New Towns were not wide enough to cope with the increase in car ownership in the 1960s. Later New Towns, such as Milton Keynes, have tried to correct some of the mistakes but it takes time for a new settlement to become properly established and to develop a character of its own.

Fig 116   Stevenage town centre

Fig 117   Residential area, Stevenage

ENQUIRY

1   Which New Towns are associated with the following conurbations/major urban areas? London; Birmingham; Liverpool/Manchester; Tyneside; Clydeside; and Belfast?
2   What was the total population of London's New Towns in 1981? (Do not include Corby in this total.)
3   Which two of the 'Main Aims and Objectives of New Towns' (Fig 114) do you think were most likely to improve the quality of life of the people moving to them, and why?
4   What advantages does the situation of Stevenage offer to light manufacturing industry?
5   In what ways does the plan of Stevenage follow the aims and objectives of New Towns mentioned in Fig 114?

6   What features of Stevenage's town centre (Fig 116) are characteristic of New Towns?
7   Describe the residential housing shown in Fig 117.
8   What do you think have been the main advantages of the UK's New Towns?
9   What do you think have been their main disadvantages?
10   Think about what you have learnt in this section and then plan your own New Town for a target population of 100 000. You could develop this into a major piece of work by including drawings and written descriptions. You could even decide where to build it!

Managing transport systems

The importance of transport developments to the growth of towns and cities has already been mentioned. However, transport is also a major problem with a number of different aspects:

- **Road Traffic.** Average journey time across Central London in 1908 (the days of the horse) was eight miles per hour. Today, with widespread car ownership, it is 12 miles per hour. Parking is a constant problem.
- **Public Transport.** London has a highly developed public transport system – buses, trains and the Underground. Most people who travel to London use public transport and demand is greatest during the morning and evening rush hours.
- **Pedestrians.** Pedestrians have to cope with crowded pavements. Crossing the road can be a dangerous experience.

As car ownership has increased so have the ways of dealing with motorists who wish to drive to or through, the central areas of our towns and cities. One-way systems have been developed in order to keep the traffic moving. Parking has been encouraged in some places by the building of multi-storey car parks whereas in other places it is discouraged by yellow lines, wheel clamps, and traffic wardens.

There have also been major schemes like the M25 which was built to keep traffic away from Central London (Fig 119). It is 120 miles long, took eleven years to construct and cost more than £1000 million. However, it would appear that people who would not have driven into Central London before the M25 was built, are now doing so because they expect the roads to be less crowded. As a result, traffic congestion is still a problem.

Also, parts of the M25 itself have become hopelessly overcrowded. Some blame the planners for not realising how many motorists would want to use it. Others blame the motorway itself for being too successful at attracting traffic. As a consequence, in 1993 plans were announced to widen its busiest sections to eight lanes.

Fig 118 Traffic jam in the Cromwell Road, London

Fig 119 The M25 near Uxbridge

Public transport is very important in our towns and cities and many people think that it should be given greater attention. Lanes for 'buses only' have been created but it only takes one parked car to slow things down. 'Park-and-ride' schemes have been set up to encourage motorists to 'park' on the outskirts and 'ride' in to the Centre on a bus. London has its Underground system and this has been developed in other conurbations as well e.g. Tyneside.

Cyclists in a big town or city can often travel at a faster speed than cars or buses. In Stevenage, cycleways and walkways have been completely separated from main roads in parts of the town (Fig 120).

For the pedestrian the traffic-free shopping area has been a major improvement. There are an increasing number of specially designed precincts, like the one in Stevenage, and also more High Streets are being **pedestrianised**, which means that they are turned into traffic-free zones. Zebra crossings, pelican crossings, and subways also help to make city centres safe for pedestrians.

Fig 120   Cycle lane and walkway, Stevenage

ENQUIRY

1   Why should traffic congestion be a particular problem in the central area of a town or city? (Think about the functions of the CBD, where it is, and when the central areas of many towns and cities were built.)
2   Why do you think widespread car ownership has only speeded up traffic in Central London by four miles per hour?
3   What problem does the rush hour present for those in charge of London's public transport system? (Think in particular about the uneven demand for public transport.)
4   Read this section again and then make a list of all the ways in which planners have tried to deal with the problem of traffic congestion.

5   For your town, or a town near you, make a list of the ways in which it tries to keep the traffic moving and to make the town centre safe for pedestrians.
6   Consider, and then write about, a pedestrianised scheme from the point of view of the following people:
  – a family shopping on a Saturday morning;
  – a lorry driver delivering to a supermarket which has its own delivery bay;
  – a lorry driver delivering to a sports shop which does not have its own delivery bay;
  – a disabled driver;
  – a traffic warden.

2.8 Why do so many of us live in towns and cities?

The earliest evidence for towns and cities has been found in present day Iraq between the Rivers Tigris and Euphrates and dates back to 4000 BC. These early towns and cities were not very big. Babylon, mentioned in the Old Testament, must have been one of the largest and probably had a population of no more than 80 000 people. However, the percentage of the world's population living in urban areas remained very small until the beginning of the nineteenth century. The rapid increase which has taken place since then (Fig 121) represents one of the biggest changes in the way people live in the last 200 years.

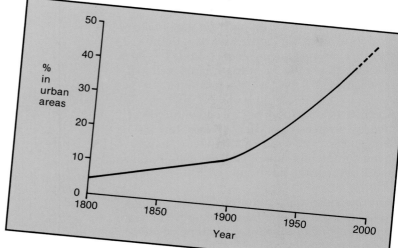

Fig 121   World urbanisation

Region	%	Region	%
Africa	30	Central America	64
China	26	South America	74
former USSR	66	Europe	75
Asia	34	Australasia	71
North America	75		

Fig 122   Urban population (i) by world region

%
70 and above

40–69

39 and below

(ii) key and shading technique

ENQUIRY

1   Use the statistics in Fig 122 (i) to draw a choropleth (shading) map to show the world pattern of urbanisation. A suggested key and shading technique is given in Fig 122 (ii).
2   Describe the pattern shown on your map.
3   Read through the following list of facts about urban areas. Re-write it as a 'diamond nine' (Fig 123) with what you think is the main advantage at the top and the main disadvantage at the bottom. The other points should be arranged in rank order. Compare your diamond nine with those of the rest of the class and discuss any similarities and differences.
    – they have a large workforce near at hand;

    – their streets and pavements can be very congested;
    – as they grow they swallow up farmland;
    – they represent a major market for anyone who wants to sell a good or market a service;
    – they have more job opportunities compared with rural areas;
    – they have to rely on rural areas for their food supplies;
    – they provide an ideal centre for Government and administration;
    – they can be very unhealthy because of overcrowding and pollution;
    – they can offer a wide range of social amenities e.g. education, entertainments.

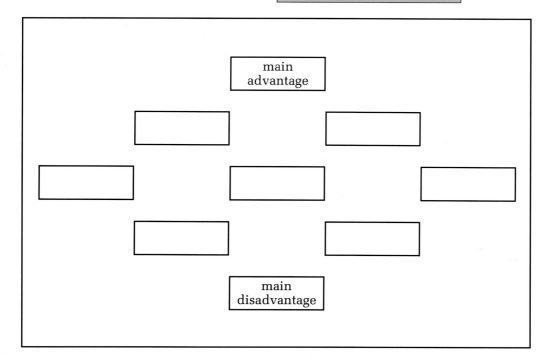

	main advantage	

Fig 123 Diamond nine

Urbanisation in England and Wales

The process by which an increasing percentage of a country's population comes to live in towns and cities is known as **urbanisation**. The two main reasons why this happens are:

● if life expectancy is greater in the urban areas than it is in the rural areas;
● if rural-urban migration is greater than urban-rural migration.

In England and Wales the major period of urbanisation was in the nineteenth century (Fig 124). However, for the first half of the century life expectancy in urban areas was lower than in the rural areas because of the extremely poor conditions found in the towns and cities (Fig 125). Houses were overcrowded; they were close to the new factories which were often a source of pollution. Sanitary provision was almost non-existent and refuse disposal was totally unsatisfactory. There were cholera epidemics

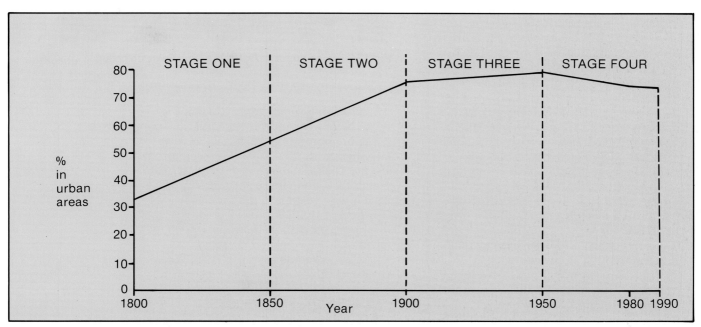

Fig 124 Urbanisation in England and Wales

in 1831, 1848 and 1866 because of polluted water, and other diseases such as smallpox were common. Consequently, the main reason for urbanisation at this time was migration from the rural areas.

In the second half of the nineteenth century conditions improved. The first Public Health Act was passed in 1848, and the first Sanitary Act in 1866. After 1870 central and local government played much more of a role in making sure that existing areas were fit to be lived in and that new areas were built to a satisfactory standard. As a result of these measures, and due to improvements in medical knowledge, life expectancy in the towns and cities improved and they began to grow as a result of **natural increase** as well as rural-urban migration.

In the first half of the twentieth century the percentage of the population living in urban areas became stable and it is now beginning to fall because of urban-rural migration (see pages 72 to 73).

Fig 125   A Newcastle slum about 1880

ENQUIRY

1   Copy Fig 124. Write these labels onto it in the correct 'stage':
  – urban population levels out;
  – lower life expectancy than in the rural areas, urbanisation because of rural-urban migration;
  – urban population begins to decline because of urban-rural migration;
  – urban growth because of rural-urban migration and natural increase.

2   Conditions were very unpleasant in the growing towns of England and Wales in the nineteenth century so there must have been good reasons why so many people moved to them. Which of the following statements were push factors (forcing people out of the rural areas) and which were pull factors (attracting people to the urban areas)?
  – the new factories of the industrial revolution needed a large number of workers;
  – rural overpopulation was causing unemployment and poverty;
  – the growing towns and cities seemed to offer a more attractive life with more things to do, more people to meet, and a better chance of 'doing well';

Fig 126   Food imports: Australian lamb being unloaded in London

  – new types of machinery meant that fewer farm workers were needed.
3   Food for urban areas has to be supplied from rural areas. For each of the next list of statements explain why it meant more food for urban areas in England and Wales in the nineteenth century.
  – improvements in methods of farming;
  – improvements in transport between rural and urban areas e.g. the railways;
  – improvements in transport between continents e.g. the invention of 'refrigeration ships'.

Urbanisation in India

The number of people living in towns and cities in India went up from 79 million (18 per cent of the total population) in 1961 to 217 million (25.7 per cent of the total population) in 1991.

Natural increase has been an important part of this process, accounting for 45 per cent of the absolute increase in the period 1971-81, and 60 per cent in the period 1981-91. It has contributed to the relative increase as well, because infant mortality rates have been much lower in the cities than in the countryside at 60 deaths per 1000 births compared with 139 deaths per 1000 births.

However, rural-urban migration has been the main factor. People have left the countryside for a variety of reasons which can be seen in terms of push and pull factors. Push factors are the ones that force people to move from a place e.g. drought. Pull factors are ones that attract people to a place e.g. a job.

A study of rural-urban migrants in Calcutta revealed drought, the chance of a better income, greater access to medical facilities and schools, and freedom from traditional village customs to be the main reasons for leaving their homes.

Many rural-urban migrants move straight to a big town or city. Others go to a small town first and move to a bigger town when they are more used to the urban way of life: this is known as 'step migration'. More recently, there has been a growth in 'circular migration' which involves leaving the village for up to eight or nine months of the year but returning home for the remainder. This has come about mainly because of improvements in transport; for example, the percentage of 'A' class roads linking towns and villages in India increased from 25 per cent in 1971 to 41 per cent in 1988. These different types of movement are summarised in Fig 127.

Until recently, most rural-urban migrants were young men. They tended to join friends and relations who were already living in the city. Once established, they found their own place to live and then arranged for their family to join them.

However, this pattern has begun to change. Firstly, many circular migrants are older men who are unable to find work in their villages; they live in hostels, and send much of their money back home, as they have no intention of staying permanently. Secondly, there has been an increase in the number of young women who are migrating because there is a demand for cheap female labour in the growing number of factories. In LEDCs as a whole, there are now more women than male migrants in the 16-25 age group, although it would appear that many of these return to their villages when they get married.

The rate of urbanisation has been so great that few towns and cities have been able to keep pace with it and squatter settlements are almost universal. For example, in common with India's other main towns and cities, Calcutta (see Section 2.4) has over 75 per cent of its population living in slums or bustees; over 60 per cent of families living in one room; and as many as 25 people sharing one tap and toilet (Fig 128).

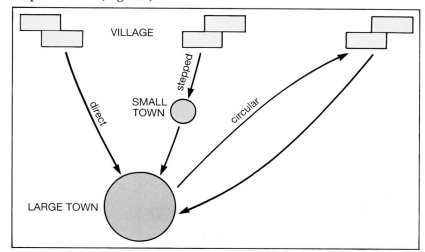

Fig 127   Types of rural-urban migration

Fig 128   Rambagan slum in Calcutta

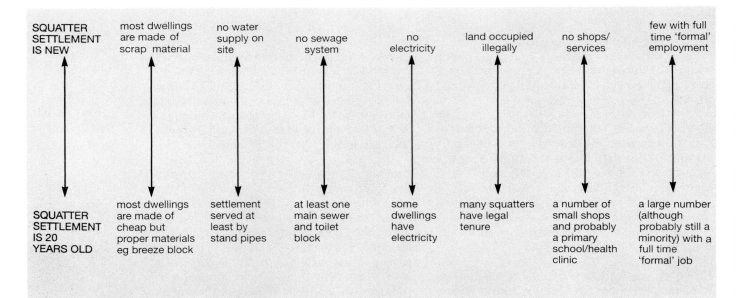

Fig 129   Squatter settlements: improvement over time

Different ways of dealing with this problem have been tried. Some squatter settlements have been removed by force but the occupants have simply moved to another part of the city. Rural development schemes have been set up to improve employment opportunities in the countryside. These tend to be expensive but there is some evidence that, overall, they are having an effect; for example, nearly 6000 'rural service centres' had been set up by the Indian Government by 1989, and the countryside's share of those officially classified as poor, fell from around 50 per cent to 30 per cent between 1977-8 and 1987-8.

New housing has been built but even the cheapest dwellings tend to be far too expensive for the rural-urban migrant. Site and service schemes have become more popular. These range from laying on water and sewage and letting the migrants build there own properties with anything they can afford, to building the shell of the house itself. However, the number who have benefited compared to the scale of the problem is relatively small.

Most improvements to squatter settlements have come about through the hard work of the people who live there, and there is plenty of evidence of conditions improving over time (Fig 129). This fact is often used by urban authorities as a reason for doing nothing.

The future for towns and cities in India looks uncertain. Fig 130 shows that the rate of urbanisation has slowed down but is still above three per cent a year. Even if this trend continues the population of towns and cities will be increasing for many years to come and they already have huge problems to deal with. India's biggest cities – Bombay, Calcutta, Delhi and Madras – appear to have reached saturation point and it seems likely that the smaller towns near these will grow instead. The countryside looks as if it is in a better position to keep people, but as the Green Revolution spreads, the number of landless peasants is likely to rise (see Section 5.3), so poor harvests or an increase in mechanisation could produce a new flood of migrants. It is by no means certain that India, or other LEDCs, will go through the same stages of urbanisation as those identified for MEDCs (see Fig 124, page 81).

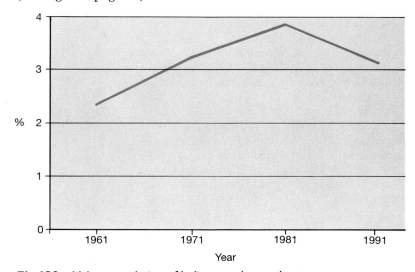

Fig 130   Urban population of India: annual growth rate

ENQUIRY

1 How important has natural increase been to the process of urbanisation in India?

2 List onto a copy of Fig 131, in their correct column, the reasons why people have moved from the countryside to Calcutta.

3 What are the main differences between the types of migration shown in Fig 127?

4 How and why has the type of person who is migrating changed in recent years?

5 What are some of the consequences of rural-urban migration for **a)** the urban areas and **b)** the rural areas?

6 What typical characteristics of squatter settlements can be seen in Fig 128?

7 Consider the advantages and disadvantages of the different ways of dealing with the squatter problem, and then complete a copy of Fig 132. Which of these strategies do you think is best, and why?

8 Do you think India's urban problems are likely to get better or worse in the next ten years? Justify your answer.

	Advantages	Disadvantages
Squatters removed by force. Settlement pulled down.		
Government build low cost housing.		
Site and service schemes.		
Rural development schemes.		

Fig 132   Solving the squatter problem: summary table

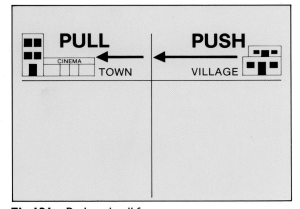

Fig 131   Push and pull factors

Million cities

In the LEDCs the rate of urbanisation has increased dramatically since the 1960s; currently it is over three per cent a year. Natural increase has been important to this process because although conditions are very poor in many of these towns and cities, there is better access to modern medicine than in the rural areas and as a result life expectancy is higher. As a consequence, many towns and cities in LEDCs have missed out stage one of Fig 124, page 81. However, rural-urban migration is the most important factor with an estimated 3000 people migrating to the cities every hour.

Over one third of this growth is taking place in towns and cities of between 20 000 and 100 000 people but an interesting aspect of urbanisation in LEDCs is the rapid increase in the number of **million cities** – cities with a population of more than one million (Figs 133 and 134). Of the largest cities of all – those with more than ten million people – it is estimated that 80 per cent will be in the LEDCs by the year 2000 (Fig 135).

Two main reasons help to explain this. Firstly, when the process of urbanisation began in MEDCs in the nineteenth century they already had a network of small towns for migrants to choose between. However, when urbanisation began in the LEDCs most of them had only a few towns, most of which had been set up during the colonial period as ports and administration centres, so migrants had very little choice of where to go. Secondly, the rate of urbanisation has been so rapid in most LEDCs that there has not been enough time for an urban network to develop.

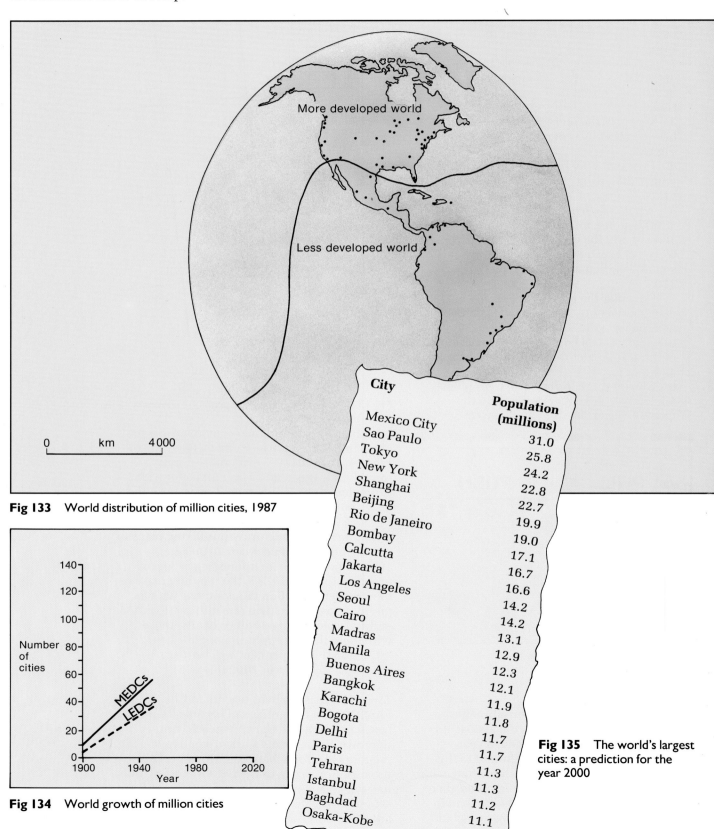

Fig 133   World distribution of million cities, 1987

Fig 134   World growth of million cities

City	Population (millions)
Mexico City	31.0
Sao Paulo	25.8
Tokyo	24.2
New York	22.8
Shanghai	22.7
Beijing	19.9
Rio de Janeiro	19.0
Bombay	17.1
Calcutta	16.7
Jakarta	16.6
Los Angeles	14.2
Seoul	14.2
Cairo	13.1
Madras	12.9
Manila	12.3
Buenos Aires	12.1
Bangkok	11.9
Karachi	11.8
Bogota	11.7
Delhi	11.7
Paris	11.3
Tehran	11.3
Istanbul	11.2
Baghdad	11.1
Osaka-Kobe	11.1

Fig 135   The world's largest cities: a prediction for the year 2000

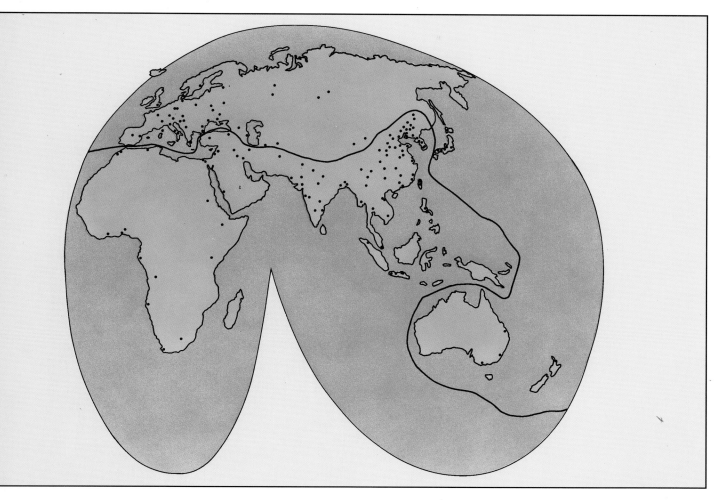

ENQUIRY

1 Look at Fig 133. How many 'million cities' are there in the MEDCs and how many in the LEDCs? Use this information to complete a copy of the graph in Fig 134.

2 What was the total number of 'million cities' in **a)** 1900 and **b)** 1980?

3 What percentage of 'million cities' were in the LEDCs in **a)** 1900 and **b)** 1980?

4 Extend the lines on your graph to the year 2020 by continuing the present trend. What is your prediction for the number of 'million cities' in 2020 and what is the balance between the MEDCs and the LEDCs?

5 Use the figures you have worked out for the above questions to help you to describe and explain the distribution of million cities past, present and future.

6 What do you notice about the distribution of the world's largest cities in Fig 135? Can you suggest an explanation?

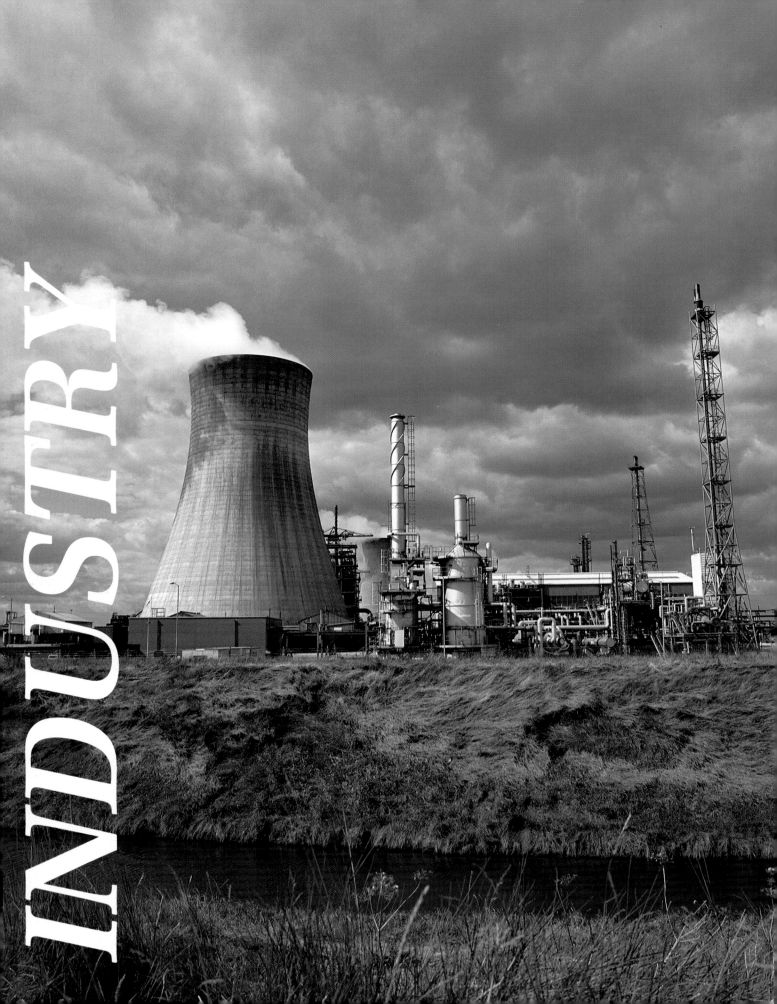

INDUSTRY

3.1 Which job goes into which category?

'Industry' means any type of work people do in order to make a living. There are so many different types of job that it is necessary to put them into groups or families.

Primary, secondary, tertiary or quaternary?

Primary industries are extractive industries which means that they get raw materials from the ground, the sea or the air. **Secondary** industries are manufacturing industries which means that they make things. **Tertiary** industries provide a service – for example, a shop keeper provides a service by selling goods and a doctor provides a service by caring for people who are ill. **Quaternary** industries are a type of service industry – they carry out research and/or use modern technology to provide specialist information and advice; market researchers or financial advisers are examples.

Grouping industries in this way makes it easy to explore the link between providing the raw materials (primary industry), turning these raw materials into a finished product (secondary industry), and selling/marketing them (tertiary/quaternary industry).

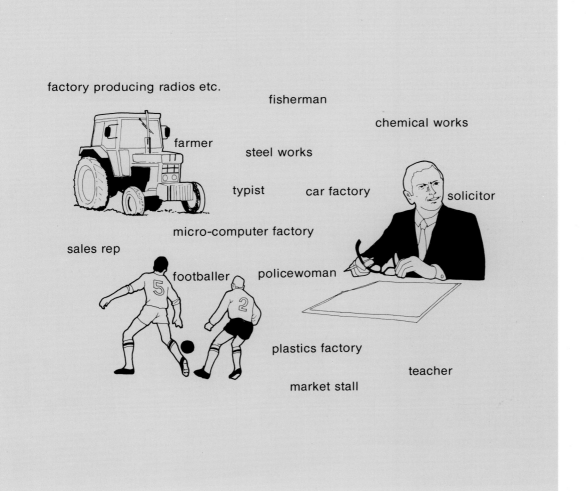

factory producing radios etc.

fisherman

chemical works

farmer

steel works

typist   car factory   solicitor

micro-computer factory

sales rep

footballer   policewoman

plastics factory

teacher

market stall

Fig 136   Types of work

Heavy or light?

This is a way of dividing up secondary (manufacturing) industry. **Heavy industries** use heavy, bulky raw materials and produce heavy, bulky goods. On the other hand **light industries** use light, small raw materials and their finished products are also light and small.

Dividing up secondary industry in this way is useful because heavy and light industries are found in different places and they have a very different impact on their surroundings. However, it can be difficult to decide on the cut-off point between what is a heavy industry and what is a light industry.

Fixed or footloose?

This grouping is to do with an industry's location – where it is found. A **fixed industry** is one that has hardly any choice in its location – for example, it may rely on a very heavy raw material so it will be near this in order to cut down transport costs. However, a **footloose industry** has no such ties and can locate in any one of a large number of places – for example, its raw materials may be light and small and therefore cheap to transport so any site with good road communications and a labour supply will be suitable.

Grouping industry in this way helps us to answer some important questions, such as where different types of industry are found and why.

1   Explain what is meant by the word 'industry'.
2   For each of the different jobs/ industries shown in Fig 136 decide whether it is an example of primary, secondary or tertiary industry. The best way to record your answers would be in a table with four columns.
3   Which of the jobs/industries in Fig 136 are examples of heavy industry and which are examples of light industry?
4   Which of the jobs/industries in Fig 136 are examples of fixed industry and which are examples of footloose industry?
5   Try to think of two more examples for each of the types of industry mentioned in this section.

Fig 137　Heavy industry: Margam steel works, Port Talbot

Fig 138　Light industry: Huntingdon in Cambridgeshire

3.2 What explains a country's occupational structure?

Occupational structure in the UK

Occupational structure means the percentage of people employed in the main categories of industry described in the previous section. It changes as a country develops and it varies from one country to another.

Fig 139 shows the changes which have taken place in the UK's occupational structure since 1800. In the nineteenth century, more people were needed to work in the towns because of the growing number of factories, while more efficient ways of farming and new farm machines meant that fewer people were needed to work on the land. As a result, the percentage of people employed in secondary industry grew while the percentage of people employed in primary industry fell. The growth of manufacturing industry led to an increase in wealth which in turn led to a greater demand for services such as health and education; as a result the tertiary sector grew.

However, in the last 30 years manufacturing industry has declined. This has happened because of a number of reasons, including the introduction of high technology labour-saving machinery and increased foreign competition. At the same time, the tertiary sector has expanded because of the growth in 'producer services' – those which serve other

organisations e.g. by providing business information, financial advice or staff training – and because of the increased demand for 'consumer services' such as shops and leisure activities.

Briefly describe and explain the main changes in the UK's occupational structure since 1800. What does the current trend suggest for the future?

Occupational structure and economic development

Fig 140 gives the occupational structure and GNP for a number of MEDCs and LEDCs. Generally, tertiary industry is the largest sector in the economy and primary industry is the smallest in MEDCs, whereas primary or tertiary industries are the largest sectors and secondary industry is the smallest in LEDCs.

It is tempting to conclude from these statistics that LEDCs should follow the example of the MEDCs and develop their manufacturing sectors in order to create wealth and improve

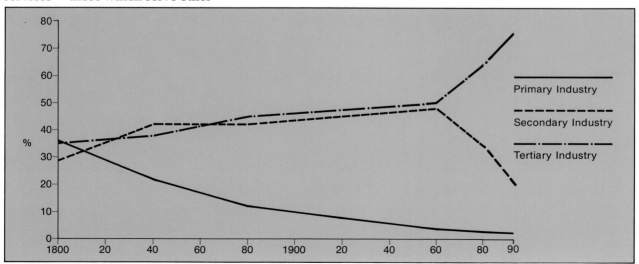

Fig 139   The UK's changing occupational structure

standards of living. However, this is not necessarily the case (see Section 5).

In fact, the occupational structures of MEDCs are already developing in a different way to the experience of the MEDCs. Fig 140 shows that many of them, for example Peru and Nigeria have much higher tertiary than secondary sectors. If you compare this with Fig 139 you can see that it is only in recent years that the UK's tertiary sector has outstripped the secondary sector.

Part of the explanation is that although the rural-urban migrants who are moving to the main towns and cities in large numbers hope to get a 'formal' full-time job e.g. in a factory, most are unsuccessful, so they have to make a living in the **informal sector** of the economy in jobs such as street-trading (Fig 141), shoe-shining or luggage-carrying. In comparison, the rural-urban migrants in the UK in the nineteenth century worked in the newly set up factories.

The main differences between the formal and informal sectors of the economy are shown in Fig 142. In reality, the two sectors overlap; for example, a street seller with a licence from the government would be officially classified in the formal sector but if they were working illegally – which is usually the case – they would be placed in the informal sector. The two sectors are also linked; for example, a factory which recycles paper relies, in part, on the urban poor who make a living by collecting waste paper.

It has been estimated that up to 90 per cent of the working population of cities in LEDCs work in the informal sector and therefore cannot guarantee a regular income, or even a living wage. This points to the need to lift people from the informal to the formal sector of the urban economy if the standard of living in cities is to be improved.

	% employed in			GNP US$ per person)
	Primary	**Secondary**	**Tertiary**	
MEDCs				
UK	2	20	78	16 750
USA	3	18	79	22 560
Japan	7	24	69	26 920
Germany	4	30	66	23 650
France	7	20	73	20 600
Spain	11	21	68	12 460
LEDCs				
India	63	11	26	330
Bangladesh	57	10	33	220
Brazil	29	16	55	2920
China	74	14	12	370
Peru	35	12	53	1020
Nigeria	45	4	51	290

Fig 140   Occupational structures and GNP

Fig 141   Fruit seller, India

ENQUIRY

1 Draw a scattergraph to show the relationship between the percentage of people employed in secondary industry and per capita GNP. Describe and try to explain the relationship you have plotted.

2 What do you think is the most important difference between the formal and the informal sector of the urban economy? Explain your choice.

3 Give three examples of jobs for each of the sectors.

4 What do you think are the advantages and disadvantages of selling fruit on the streets, like the woman in Fig 141? Consider this question from the point of view of the seller, the customer and the urban authorities.

5 Which of the following ways to encourage the formal sector do you think would be best, and why?
● offer low interest loans to small businesses;
● organise a proper market place for street sellers;
● set up a government-run factory.

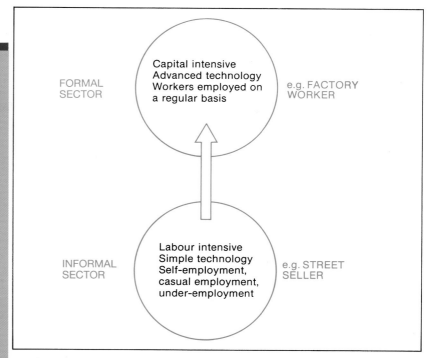

Fig 142   The formal and informal sectors of a developing economy

Fig 143   Working in the informal service sector

Women and work

Women in MEDCs have more opportunities than women in LEDCs. For example, boys and girls in MEDCs have the same chance of going to school whereas in many LEDCs far fewer girls go to school than boys. However, there are still differences in the jobs that women do. Some of these are shown in Fig 144.

Also, recent years have seen an increase in the number of part-time jobs (Fig 145), most of which are taken by women. The work, such as shelf-filling in supermarkets, tends to require few skills and the pay is generally low. Many of these jobs are in the evenings and at the weekends, and women do them as well as their domestic chores.

Attempts have been made to raise awareness of the importance of women to the economies of EDCs; for example, the United Nations organised a 'Decade for Women' between 1975 and 1985. Statistics like the ones in Fig 146 show how important women are to world productivity. Given the major role women already play it seems sensible that they should be a major consideration in any development strategy. Julius Nyerere, Tanzania's first President, illustrated this point by saying, "*A person does not walk very far or very fast on one leg, so how can we expect half the people to develop a nation?*"

Changes have taken place but they have not always been for the better. For example, the percentage of women in the workforce has risen, especially in the 'Newly Industrialising Countries' **(NICs)** (Fig 148), but the jobs these women are doing tend to be low-paid with long hours, little security and very poor working conditions. Also, these jobs tend to be in addition to looking after their homes and families.

However, there have been successes. Fig 149 shows a project in eastern Thailand which was funded by Population Concern, a UK charity, and the EU. Women's groups were set up growing mushrooms. They were given training in production, management and marketing skills. They were also given education about home management, nutrition, child care and family planning, the aim being to improve the overall quality of their lives and not just their income. The money earnt from the sale of the mushrooms has given them a new importance because

a) Men

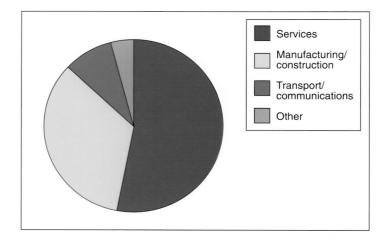

b) Women

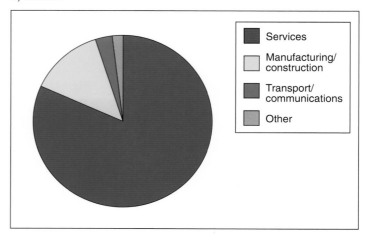

Fig 144 Employment in the UK, 1994

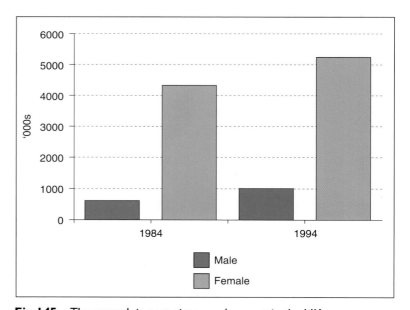

Fig 145 The growth in part-time employment in the UK

they are now wage earners. As a result they have been able to take more of a part in family decisions which affect their lives.

Schemes like this one are only a start and affect a relatively small number of women. However, they indicate the sort of strategy that could be part of an overall development programme.

Fig 147   Half the people . . .

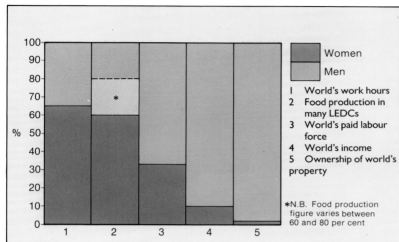

Women
Men
1 World's work hours
2 Food production in many LEDCs
3 World's paid labour force
4 World's income
5 Ownership of world's property

*N.B. Food production figure varies between 60 and 80 per cent

Fig 146   Women's responsibilities

	% of women in the workforce		% of women employed in the manufacturing sector (1970s)
	1970	1980	
South Korea	26	30	41
Taiwan	27	34	48
Hong Kong	43	50	54
Singapore	30	44	41
Malaysia	28	45	35
Thailand	45	54	24
Philippines	34	n/a	24
Indonesia	26	28	24

Fig 148   Women's role in the workforce

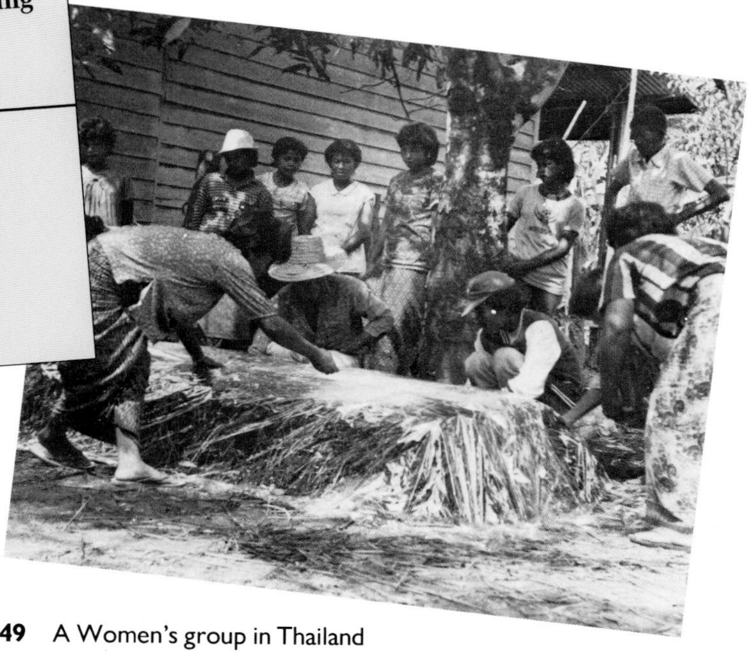

Fig 149   A Women's group in Thailand

1   What do the pie charts in Fig 144 tell us about employment in the UK?

2   Describe the trend shown in Fig 145. what are its consequences – good and bad for women in MEDCs?

3   Study Fig 146. Write a paragraph about what it shows.

4   Look at Fig 148. Describe what this graph shows. Why do statistics such as these not necessarily represent an improvement for women?

5   What do you think are the advantages and the disadvantages of a scheme like the one which has been set up in eastern Thailand?

6   There are many different attitudes about the role of women in society. Some examples include: "Women should be treated the same as men and should have the same chances in life"; "Women are different to men and can never be equal"; "A woman's place is in the home and a man's place is at work"; "A woman can do any job as well as a man – if not better". What do you think the role of women should be? Explain your opinion.

3.3 *What about the unemployed?*

The occupational structures looked at in the last section gave information about people in work. However, all countries have people who are unemployed.

Unemployment in the UK

Fig 150 shows how the unemployment rate has changed since 1986 and Fig 151 shows that some parts of the country have a higher rate of unemployment than others. However, the situation is more complex than these statistics suggest.

Firstly, there are important structural differences. For example, Fig 152 shows that between 1979 and 1986 most job losses were in secondary industry but that jobs in tertiary industry actually increased.

Secondly, there are big variations within each region. For example, Fig 153 shows how rich and poor people live alongside each other on Teeside while unemployment in London's inner city is often more than 20 per cent.

Thirdly, unemployment can also be broken down by ethnic origin. For example, Fig 154 shows that, particularly for young people, the unemployment rate among the UK's ethnic minorities is above the national average.

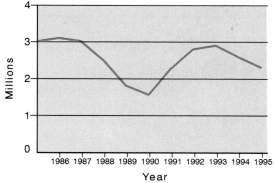

Fig 150   Employment changes in the UK since 1981

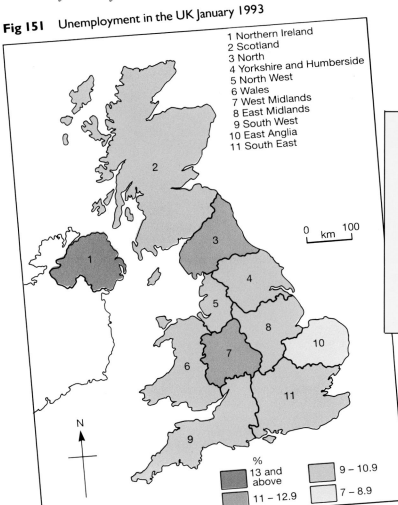

Fig 151   Unemployment in the UK January 1993

1 Northern Ireland
2 Scotland
3 North
4 Yorkshire and Humberside
5 North West
6 Wales
7 West Midlands
8 East Midlands
9 South West
10 East Anglia
11 South East

0   km   100

N

%
13 and above
11 – 12.9
9 – 10.9
7 – 8.9

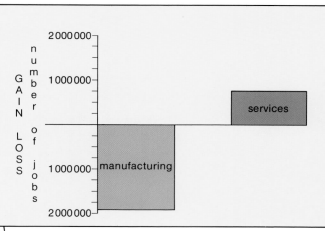

Fig 152   Changes in employment 1979-1986

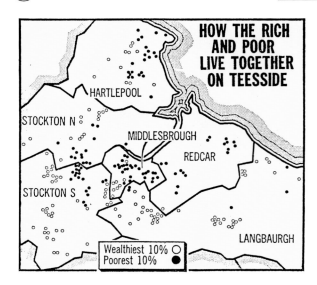

Fig 153 How the rich and poor live together on Teesside

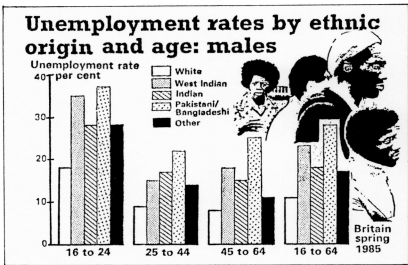

Fig 154 Unemployment rates by ethnic origin and age: males

In the 1980s the north of the country had a net loss of jobs while the south had a net gain (Fig 155). This was mainly because the north had a larger manufacturing sector and most of the jobs lost during this period were in secondary industry. On the other hand, the south has always had a larger service sector and most of

the jobs gained were in tertiary industry. This led to concern about a 'north-south divide' with the north of the country becoming poorer and the south of the country becoming richer.

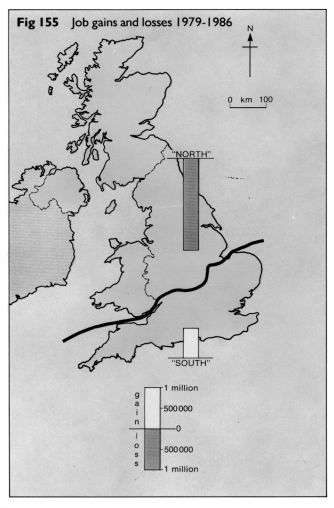

Fig 155 Job gains and losses 1979-1986

	Service sector		Manufacturing	
	'000s	%	'000s	%
South East	−329	−5.9	−154	−13.8
East Anglia	−13	−2.4	−16	−9.7
South West	−4	−0.3	−51	−15.8
West Midlands	−21	−1.7	−104	−18.2
East Midlands	+20	+2.1	−39	−8.8
Yorks and Humberside	−13	−1.1	−40	−8.7
North West	+10	+0.6	−74	−12.9
North	−3	−0.4	−18	−7.1
Wales	−10	−1.5	−21	−9.5
Scotland	+68	+4.8	−31	−8.4
Northern Ireland	+2	+0.5	−7	−7.1

Fig 156 Change in service and manufacturing employment 1990-1992

However, although job losses in manufacturing industry have continued in the 1990s, there have been job losses in the service sector as well (Fig 156). Most of this decline has taken place in the south of the country and as a result the north-south divide has become less noticeable.

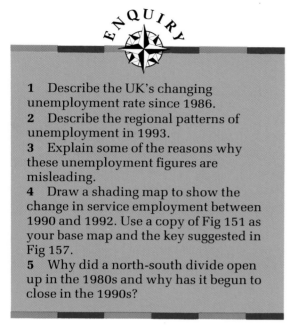

ENQUIRY

1 Describe the UK's changing unemployment rate since 1986.
2 Describe the regional patterns of unemployment in 1993.
3 Explain some of the reasons why these unemployment figures are misleading.
4 Draw a shading map to show the change in service employment between 1990 and 1992. Use a copy of Fig 151 as your base map and the key suggested in Fig 157.
5 Why did a north-south divide open up in the 1980s and why has it begun to close in the 1990s?

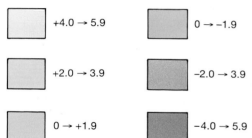

+4.0 → 5.9	0 → –1.9
+2.0 → 3.9	–2.0 → 3.9
0 → +1.9	–4.0 → 5.9

Fig 157 Key for service employment map

Aid to Industry

For many years all governments in the UK have been involved with industry. On the one hand there are planning controls and restrictions; on the other hand there is help and encouragement. It is in every government's interest to stop unemployment becoming too high because the economy suffers, social problems increase and its own popularity is put at risk – and therefore its chance of being re-elected.

Currently, industry is being helped in a number of different ways (Fig 158). Firms setting up in the Development Areas receive grants for buildings and equipment and get help with training. The Enterprise Zones are designed to help industry in specific places: firms receive benefits such as not having to pay rates for ten years and not having to get planning permission for new developments. The Urban Development Corporations have special powers to control all developments in their area; they try to encourage industry by attracting public and private investment. Further assistance comes from sources such as the EU's Regional Development Fund (see page 113) and CoSIRA (the Council for Small Industries in Rural Areas).

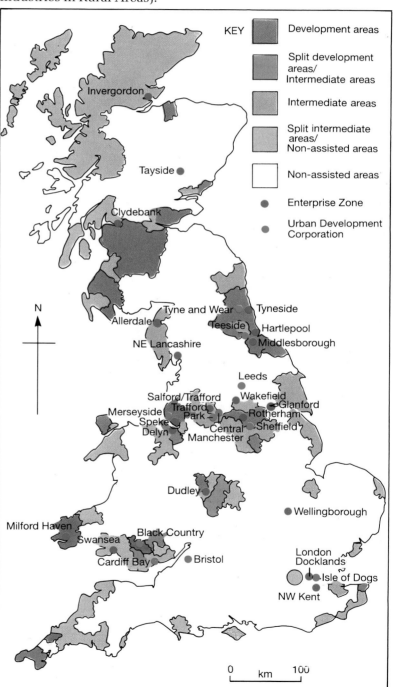

Fig 158 Aid to industry

1 Describe, and try to explain, the distribution of the Development Areas.
2 Choose one of the Enterprise Zones in the 'more prosperous' south of the country and explain why it needs help.
3 Urban Development Corporations can make things easier for industry by cutting through red tape but can you think of any disadvantages of having fewer planning controls than usual?
4 Read the points of view put forward in Fig 159. Do you think the government should give more or less help to industry? Explain your opinion.

I think the government should be more involved in helping industry.

It should spend more money on creating jobs and less money on unemployment benefit.

It should stop industry from setting up in the prosperous south.

It should move government offices to areas of high unemployment.

It should keep unprofitable industries going until there are other jobs for the workers.

The government should always buy British in order to help our own workers.

I think the government is involved enough and industry should be allowed to get on with the job itself.

It should not spend any more money creating jobs because the tax-payer cannot afford the bill.

It should have some restrictions but not too many or it will put industry off altogether.

Moving government offices is a waste of money.

Why throw good money after bad? It just delays the day when something has to be done.

It should save the tax-payer money by buying from the cheapest supplier.

Fig 159   How much help should the Government give industry?

3.4 *Why build it there?*

ICI, Stowmarket

Imperial Chemical Industries (ICI) is a large UK-based **multinational** company which means that it has factories in other countries as well as in the UK (see Section 6.3).

The Stowmarket factory is part of ICI's Paints Division. The site was first developed in 1863 with the building of an explosives factory. For transport in the early days it relied on barges using the River Gipping. Later, the railway became more important and now all its raw materials and finished products are moved by road. Stowmarket is on the A14 which links it to the port of Felixstowe, the M11, the A1 and the Midlands.

The Stowmarket factory became part of ICI (Paints) Ltd in 1940. Of ICI's 50 or so paints factories worldwide (Fig 160) it is one of the largest with a workforce of over 700, an annual production of 50 million litres of decorative paint and a resin plant opened in 1982 at a cost of £20 million.

Decorative paints are made by combining pigments and extenders (these give the paint its colour and its ability to cover a surface); resins (these give the paint many of its special qualities, such as hardness); and solvents (these control the paint's thickness and its drying speed).

The main pigment is titanium dioxide because of its exceptional whiteness and its covering power. It is obtained from rutile ore which is imported from Australia and refined on Teesside and Humberside. The extenders are china clay (kaolin) from St Austell in Cornwall, and calcium carbonate from the chalk deposits of Royston in Hertfordshire, or from France. As has been mentioned, Stowmarket has its own resin plant which also supplies other ICI paints factories both here and in Europe. The resins are made by combining solvents which come from various refineries in the UK, and chemicals known as monomers which come from the UK and also from Germany. These, together with Stowmarket's other inputs, are shown in Fig 162.

The pigments and extenders are kept in large silos and are fed into the factory along

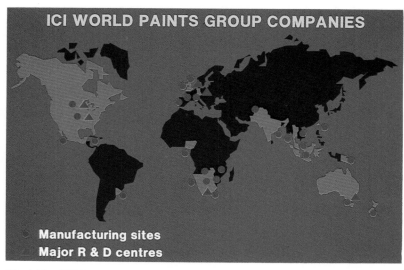

Fig 160 ICI Paints: world distribution

connecting pipes; these can be seen in Fig 163. The paint passes downwards from one floor to the next as it is processed.

Stowmarket also has a solvent recovery plant which supplies some of the fuel for the boilers.

1 On an outline map of the UK mark on and label ICI Stowmarket and the places it gets its raw materials from. (If these places are outside of the UK simply list them where you have space on your map).
2 Why is Stowmarket a good location for a factory of this type?
3 Write an account of ICI Stowmarket using the following headings:
  – size of factory;
  – equipment and machinery;
  – number of employees;
  – inputs;
  – processes;
  – outputs;
  – marketing.
4 Which of the groups of industry mentioned in Section 3.1 could this factory be put into?

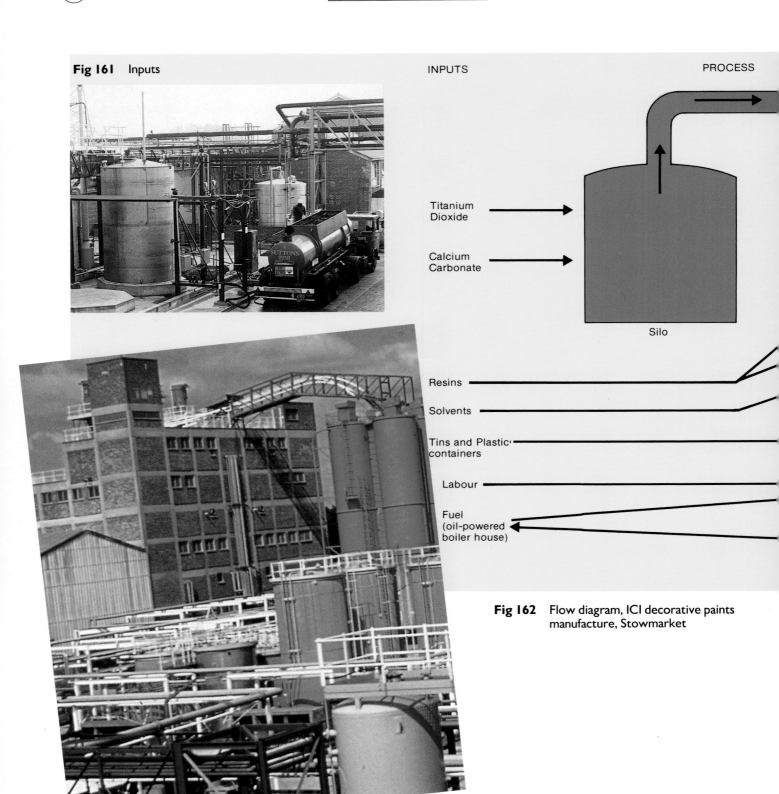

Fig 161 Inputs

INPUTS

PROCESS

Titanium
Dioxide

Calcium
Carbonate

Silo

Resins

Solvents

Tins and Plastic
containers

Labour

Fuel
(oil-powered
boiler house)

Fig 162 Flow diagram, ICI decorative paints
manufacture, Stowmarket

Fig 163 Processes

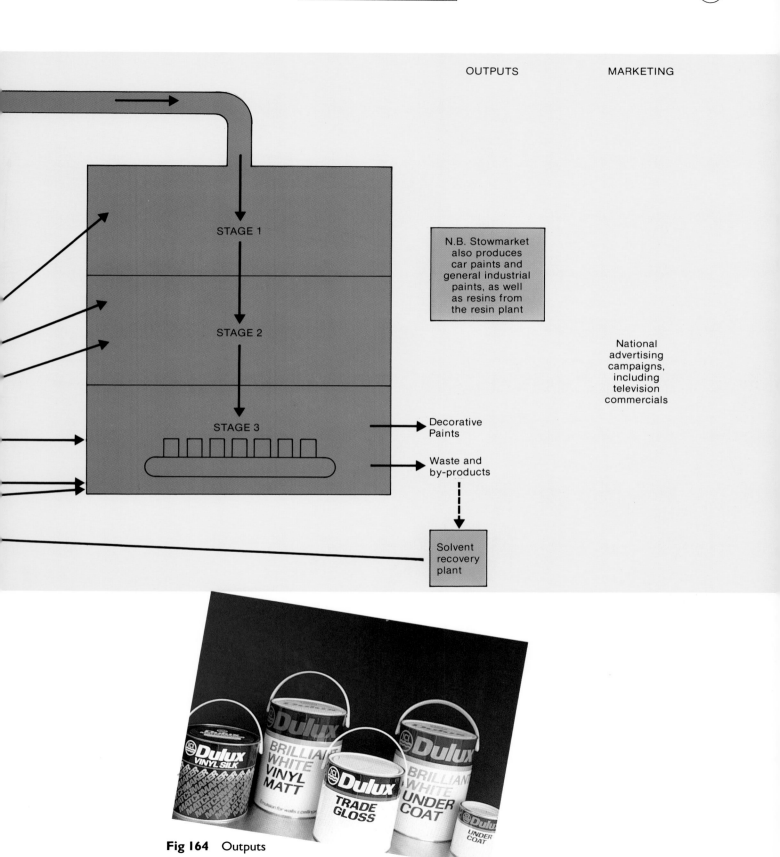

OUTPUTS   MARKETING

STAGE 1

STAGE 2

STAGE 3

N.B. Stowmarket
also produces
car paints and
general industrial
paints, as well
as resins from
the resin plant

National
advertising
campaigns,
including
television
commercials

Decorative
Paints

Waste and
by-products

Solvent
recovery
plant

Fig 164   Outputs

3.5 Why do some industries group together?

The high-technology industries and science parks

The high-technology industries (HTIs) make electronic components, precision instruments, telecommunications equipment and, in particular, computers, microchips and microprocessors. Their raw materials are light and easy to transport. Many HTI factories are 'assembly plants'; these specialise in putting together components made elsewhere. HTIs are becoming increasingly important in the UK – for example, they now provide more than 25 per cent of manufacturing jobs.

HTIs often group together (**agglomerate**) on industrial estates known as 'science parks'; for example, the Cambridge Science Park (Fig 165) was set up by Trinity College in 1973 and now has 81 companies and nearly 3000 employees.

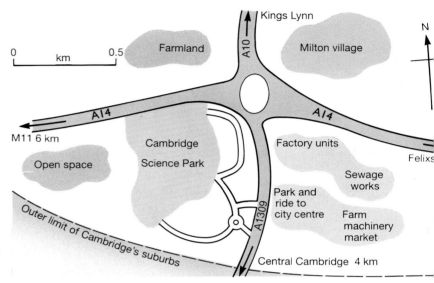

Fig 165 Cambridge Science Park

Science parks have a number of advantages.

• They can be located near to a main road on the edge of a town for easy access.
• They keep industry separated from other types of land use.
• Firms can benefit from being near each other – for example, if they supply components.
• Services and facilities such as roads, car parks and waste disposal can be planned and organised efficiently.
• The environment can be designed so that it is a pleasant place in which to work.

However, there can be disadvantages as well.

• HTIs are very competitive and some firms want to be on a site by themselves so that it is easier to keep new ideas a secret.
• There can be traffic problems, particularly during the rush hour, with vehicles trying to get in and out of the estate.
• If they are on the edge of a town the employees are a long way from the shops and services of the town centre.
• Planning applications have sometimes been turned down because the buildings do not fit in with the general appearance of the area.

HTIs are found in all regions of the UK. However, in the 1980s the number of people employed in these industries in big towns and cities fell while the number employed in small towns and rural areas increased. The main reason for this change seems to be people leaving the big towns in search of a pleasanter environment and a better quality of life; as such, it is part of the process of de-urbanisation discussed in Section 2.7.

Three areas have developed as centres of production: the M4 corridor extending into Wales; central Scotland; and the area around Cambridge (Fig 166). The M4 corridor has benefited from its good communications with London, the international links provided by Heathrow airport and its links with government research establishments e.g. at Aldermaston. The South Wales end of the corridor has also benefited from government assistance and was the second fastest-growing high-tech region in the country between 1981 and 1987 with a 21 per cent increase (7000 jobs).

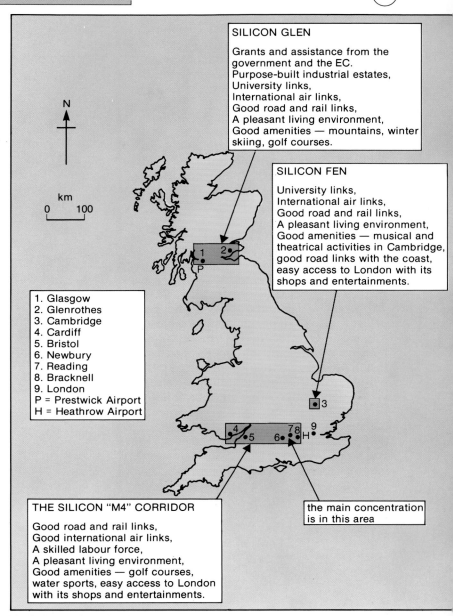

SILICON GLEN

Grants and assistance from the government and the EC.
Purpose-built industrial estates,
University links,
International air links,
Good road and rail links,
A pleasant living environment,
Good amenities — mountains, winter skiing, golf courses.

SILICON FEN

University links,
International air links,
Good road and rail links,
A pleasant living environment,
Good amenities — musical and theatrical activities in Cambridge, good road links with the coast, easy access to London with its shops and entertainments.

1. Glasgow
2. Glenrothes
3. Cambridge
4. Cardiff
5. Bristol
6. Newbury
7. Reading
8. Bracknell
9. London
P = Prestwick Airport
H = Heathrow Airport

the main concentration is in this area

THE SILICON "M4" CORRIDOR

Good road and rail links,
Good international air links,
A skilled labour force,
A pleasant living environment,
Good amenities — golf courses, water sports, easy access to London with its shops and entertainments.

Fig 166   High-technology industry

Fig 167   Hewlett-Packard

Government assistance has also been important to the development of Scotland's 'Silicon Glen', with 80 per cent of foreign-owned computer companies giving this as the major reason for locating there.

The Cambridge region, 'Silicon Fen', has benefited greatly from its links with the university: these have provided research facilities, skilled graduates and prestige. It was the fastest-growing high-tech region in the country between 1981 and 1987 with a 26 per cent increase (8000 jobs).

A concentration of HTIs brings jobs and prosperity to a region but there can be drawbacks as well. For example, Berkshire, which is at the heart of the M4 corridor, has seen its population nearly double in the last 40 years. The demand for housing has caused prices to rise to 70 per cent above the national average and has resulted in thousands of hectares of farm land and open space being lost to new developments. Increased traffic has led to congestion, pollution and a road maintenance bill costing millions of pounds (in 1988 7.5 per cent of main roads surveyed had less than a year's life left in them). Services such as water supply, waste disposal and the provision of leisure and recreation have also been put under pressure.

ENQUIRY

1   Which of the groups of industry mentioned in Section 3.1 could HTIs be put into?
2   Look at Fig 165. What are the advantages of the site, situation and layout of the Cambridge Science Park? What could be its disadvantages? What is your opinion of the design of the buildings?
3   Look at Fig 166. Where are the main centres of HTI production in the UK? For each centre state its main locational advantage (i.e. the main reason why HTIs have located there). Which locational factors are common to all of these centres?
4   What problems have concentrations of HTIs brought to some regions, and why?

3.6 How and why do industries change?

The iron and steel industry

| INPUTS | PROCESS | OUTPUTS | INPUTS | PROCESS | OUTPUTS | PROCESS | OUTPUTS |

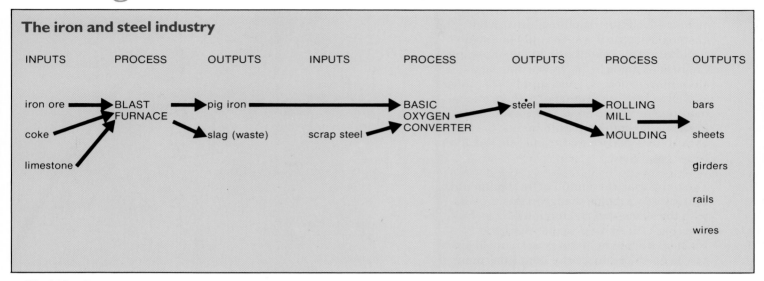

iron ore → BLAST FURNACE → pig iron → BASIC OXYGEN CONVERTER

coke → BLAST FURNACE

limestone → BLAST FURNACE

BLAST FURNACE → slag (waste)

scrap steel → BASIC OXYGEN CONVERTER

BASIC OXYGEN CONVERTER → steel → ROLLING MILL / MOULDING

ROLLING MILL / MOULDING → bars, sheets, girders, rails, wires

Fig 168   Flow diagram of an integrated iron and steel works

Iron is made by smelting iron ore in a blast furnace. Coke is used to heat the furnace and limestone is added to remove some of the impurities. The liquid iron cools and hardens to form 'pig iron' but it is brittle and hard to work, so it is either re-melted and poured into moulds to make cast iron, or it is turned into steel.

Steel is made by re-melting pig iron at a very high temperature in a converter in order to burn off the remaining impurities, and by adding small amounts of other elements to give it special properties; for example, carbon makes it easy to weld and to shape into tools, while chromium stops it from rusting.

Iron and steel used to be made in separate factories but now they are usually made in an **integrated iron and steel works** where all the processes are carried out on the one site (Fig 168).

The Margam steel works at Port Talbot in South Wales is the largest integrated works in the UK (Fig 169). The site has a number of advantages which are summarised in Fig 170. It produces three million tonnes a year mainly for motor vehicles, the building industry (e.g. steel girders) and the tinplate industry (e.g. at Swansea – coating steel with tin protects it from rust).

Fig 169   Margam steelworks, Port Talbot

Three of the UK's four remaining integrated iron and steelworks are on or near the coast (Fig 171). The main reason is the need to import large quantities of iron ore and coal.

However, the iron and steel industry has not always been located on the coast. In the early eighteenth century smelting iron ore relied on charcoal because it was the only fuel which could reach and maintain a high temperature. Charcoal is made by partly burning large amounts of wood, so good supplies of timber, as well as iron ore, were the main locational requirements. Two areas of the country, in particular, met these requirements: the Forest of Dean in Gloucestershire and The Weald in Sussex and Kent.

The Industrial Revolution of the eighteenth century saw a major change in this process with the successful production of coke from coal (Fig 172). Coke provides the same constant high temperatures as charcoal but it can be produced in greater quantities more quickly and more cheaply. This meant that supplies of coal replaced supplies of timber as a locational factor. As a result, the iron and steel industry moved to coalfields which had, or were in easy reach of, iron ore deposits. By 1800 the main areas of production were Scotland, South Wales, North East England, Yorkshire, Shropshire and the Black Country (the West Midlands).

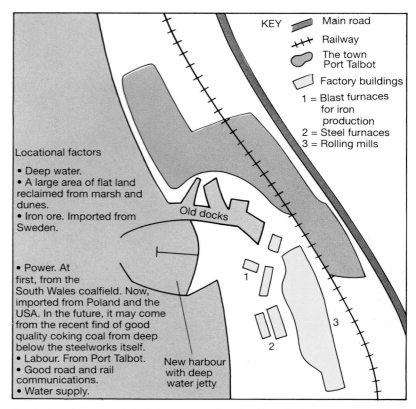

Locational factors

• Deep water.
• A large area of flat land reclaimed from marsh and dunes.
• Iron ore. Imported from Sweden.

• Power. At first, from the South Wales coalfield. Now, imported from Poland and the USA. In the future, it may come from the recent find of good quality coking coal from deep below the steelworks itself.
• Labour. From Port Talbot.
• Good road and rail communications.
• Water supply.

New harbour with deep water jetty

Fig 170   Site map of the Margam steelworks, Port Talbot

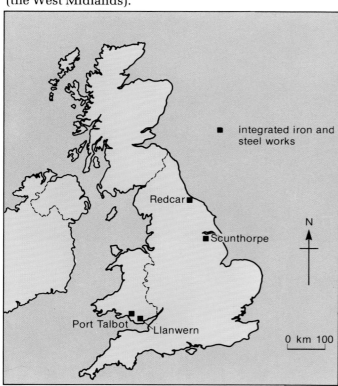

Fig 171   The UK's integrated iron and steel works

Fig 172   The Coalbrookdale furnace near Telford in Shropshire: the first to use coke to smelt iron ore

By the second half of the nineteenth century deposits of good quality iron ore were beginning to run out. The answer was to import ore from abroad and this gave coastal sites an advantage. However, some inland sites survived for over another hundred years. This was partly because they still had good supplies of coal and partly because of 'industrial inertia'. This is the term used to describe industries staying in theoretically bad locations because, for example, it is too expensive to move the factory, or because there is a skilled workforce nearby.

The post-1945 period has seen a major decline in the number of steelworks. Foreign competition, less demand for steel with the rise of plastic alternatives, and the high cost of keeping equipment up to date have all contributed to this decline. Nearly all of the inland works (most of which had run out of coking coal as well as iron ore) have closed down. The number of workers has fallen from 336 000 in 1967 to 42 000 in 1993. Production has declined from 24.7 million tonnes in 1966 to 13.8 million tonnes in 1992.

These changes have brought advantages and disadvantages; for example, closing down iron and steelworks has reduced pollution but it has also resulted in high rates of unemployment and large areas of derelict land.

Some places have coped better than others. For example, Corby, in Northamptonshire (which had been developed only in the 1950s when it became possible to use low grade deposits of iron ore found nearby) saw its unemployment rate rise to 30 per cent overnight when its steelworks was closed in 1980. However, it was able to take advantage of its central location and it attracted light industries e.g. Golden Wonder crisps and Avon Cosmetics, so that by 1988 its unemployment rate had fallen to only slightly above the national average at 11 per cent.

On the other hand, places like Merthyr Tydfil and Ebbw Vale in South Wales have had problems attracting new industries. This is largely because they are more difficult to get to and because their valley locations mean that there is very little room for industrial expansion; the new industries which have set up in the region have usually chosen sites nearer to the M4, e.g. Toshiba at Treforest (Fig 174). Events such as the Ebbw Vale Garden Festival have been set up to attract investment but they have had limited success (Fig 175).

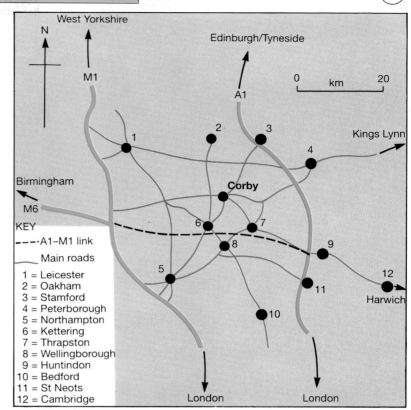

Fig 173 Corby: situation map

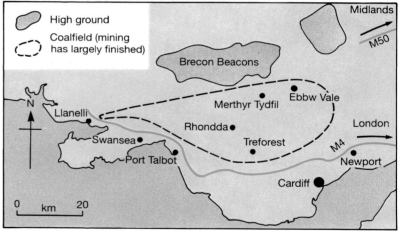

Fig 174 South Wales: situation map

Fig 175 Ebbw Vale Garden Festival 1992

ENQUIRY

1 Which of the groups of industry mentioned in Section 3.1 could an integrated iron and steelworks be put into?

2 Look at Figs 170 and 171. What are the advantages of the site and situation of the Port Talbot steelworks?

3 On an outline map of the British Isles, show the changing location of the iron and steel industry – from the forests, to the coalfields and finally to the coast. Add brief labels to explain the main reasons for each of these locations.

4 How has the iron and steel industry changed since 1945? What have some of the good and bad effects of these changes been?

5 Compare the situations of Corby and Ebbw Vale. Why is Corby more likely to attract new light industry?

6 Compare an integrated iron and steelworks with a high-technology industry (e.g. Fig 167, page 105) from the point of view of **a)** their employees and **b)** their impact on the environment.

7 Compare the location of the UK's integrated iron and steelworks with its main centres of HTI. What are the differences, and why?

8 What does Fig 176 say about the role of **a)** foreign competition and **b)** the EU in the future development of the iron and steel industry in the UK?

EC subsidies 'threaten British steel jobs'

Patrick Wintour

THE British steel industry is likely to be in for a share of the 70,000 job losses due to hit the European steel industry unless the European Community acts to stop governments writing off their domestic industry's huge debts, the House of Lords EC industry committee warns in a report published yesterday.

The peers put special blame on Italy and Spain, saying they are both openly giving subsidies to their near-bankrupt industries in breach of the Treaty of Paris – which set up the European Iron and Steel Community – but even in Germany high debt levels are encouraging steel firms and their bankers to keep inefficient plant open, rather than face closure costs.

Calling for an end to all state aid in the industry, the peers warn: 'There is a real danger that efficient private firms will suffer at the expense of uncompetitive capacity which is being artificially maintained. Excess production depresses prices and profitability hits sales and profitability throughout the industry.'

The Ravenscraig steel plant, the report claims, might not have had to close in 1992 if open and hidden subsidies elsewhere in the EC had been properly controlled.

A council of ministers is due to meet in September to try to agree an EC-wide closure programme, including fresh bans on unlawful subsidies and implementation of a three-year closure programme, backed by £340 million subsidies to close loss-making plant.

The peers warn the EC "against the temptation to ride out the current difficulties in the hope of better times as the recession ends. While the recession has undoubtedly made matters worse, the upturn will not solve the industry's structural problems."

But they say British steel is the most competitive of the EC industries, and should not be expected to take part in the imminent round of closures. Unlike many of the southern EC steel industries, the highly-profitable British industry has cut capacity by 19 per cent and reduced the workforce by 200,000 since the 1970s to 41,800.

The Guardian, 19 August 1993

Fig 176 EC subsidies 'threaten British steel jobs'

3.7 Industry in the EU – what is it like, and why?

The EU was set up in 1957 when the six original members signed the Treaty of Rome – France, West Germany, Italy, Belgium, Luxembourg and the Netherlands. In 1973 the UK, Ireland and Denmark joined; in 1981 Greece; in 1986 Spain and Portugal; and in 1995 Austria, Finland and Sweden.

The main aim of the EU is to make Europe more prosperous and a better place to live in through a degree of economic and political co-operation. Each country makes a contribution to the Union budget and four main institutions are in charge of running this budget and Union matters in general.

1 The Commission. Each country has one or two representatives according to its population. It is in charge of the day-to-day running of the Union and advises the European Parliament and the Council of Ministers.

2 The European Parliament. Each country elects members to this Parliament. It debates issues, makes recommendations to the Council of Ministers and votes on the yearly budget.

3 The Council of Ministers. Each country sends a representative but votes are weighted according to the population of the country. Nearly all final decisions are made by this body.

4 The European Court of Justice. Each country sends one judge to this court and their job is to settle disputes between member countries.

The EU has influenced industry in Europe in a number of ways. These can be summarised as follows:

• It has tried to develop common policies e.g. about the steel industry.
• It has made trade easier by removing quotas and import duties.
• It has made it possible for EU citizens to be employed in any EU country without having to get a work permit.
• It helps industry with grants from the Regional Development Fund (RDF).

However, it is difficult to say how significant its influence has been. Governments have not always agreed on common policies. Fewer trade restrictions have helped some firms, but increased competition has put others out of business. Few people have moved abroad to work (many European countries have high unemployment rates anyway). The RDF is for all types of development, not just industrial development, and although we received £424 million from the RDF in 1991 this represents a small percentage of total public expenditure.

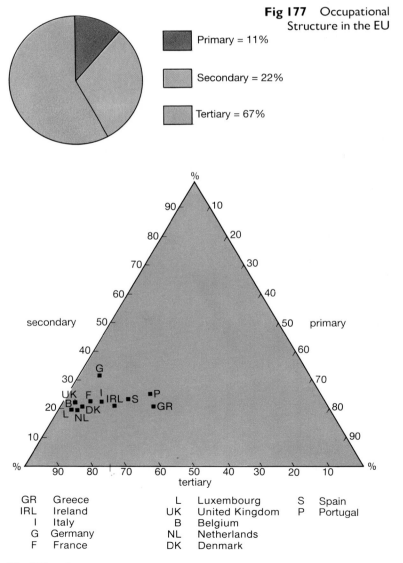

Fig 177 Occupational Structure in the EU

Primary = 11%

Secondary = 22%

Tertiary = 67%

GR	Greece	L	Luxembourg	S	Spain
IRL	Ireland	UK	United Kingdom	P	Portugal
I	Italy	B	Belgium		
G	Germany	NL	Netherlands		
F	France	DK	Denmark		

Fig 178 Occupational structure in EU countries

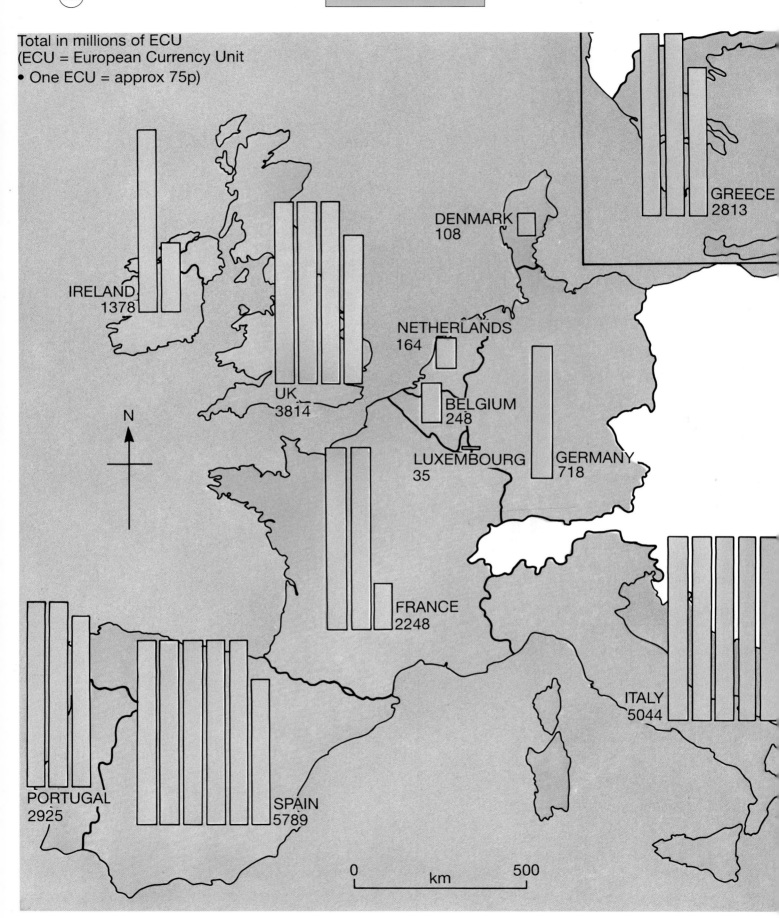

Total in millions of ECU
(ECU = European Currency Unit
• One ECU = approx 75p)

GREECE
2813

DENMARK
108

IRELAND
1378

NETHERLANDS
164

UK
3814

BELGIUM
248

LUXEMBOURG
35

GERMANY
718

N

FRANCE
2248

ITALY
5044

PORTUGAL
2925

SPAIN
5789

0   km   500

ENQUIRY

1 On an outline map of Europe shade in and label the 15 countries which make up the EU. Use different colours for the five dates when countries joined.

2 State the main aim of the EU and describe the institutions set up to run the Community.

3 Look at Fig 177. Approximately what percentage of the EU's population is employed in **a)** primary **b)** secondary and **c)** tertiary industry?

4 The overall picture hides some important differences between countries. Use the triangular graph in Fig 178 to find out the percentage of people employed in the three categories mentioned in **a)** Ireland **b)** Denmark and **c)** the UK. Describe the differences you have found. Can you think of any explanations.

5 Explain how the EU has tried to influence industrial development.

6 Why do you think it is difficult to get governments to agree to common policies?

7 Study Fig 179. List the countries in rank order according to how much they received from the RDF between 1986 and 1991. Put the country which has received most at the top of your list.

8 Compare the grants these countries have received with their population. Are there any surprises where a country seems to get much more or much less than its population would suggest? Can you think of any explanations?

Country	Population
Germany	77.60
Italy	57.10
UK	57.20
France	56.10
Netherlands	15.00
Belgium	9.80
Greece	10.00
Denmark	5.10
Ireland	3.70
Luxembourg	0.40
Spain	39.20
Portugal	10.3

(in millions, 1991 estimate)

Fig 180 Population of EU countries

Fig 179 Assistance from the European Regional Development Fund 1986-1991

3.8 Assessment task: *Manufacturing industry in the USA*

The development of manufacturing industry in the USA took off in the last quarter of the nineteenth century and by 1945 it was one of the world's leading industrial nations (see Fig 241, page 151). In recent years manufacturing has lost ground to service industries but it still accounts for 21 per cent of the country's **GDP** and in the last ten years the number of people employed in manufacturing has actually risen.

Manufacturing industry is found throughout the USA but there are two regions – the **Manufacturing Belt** and the **Sunbelt** – where it is particularly important (Fig 181). The Manufacturing Belt is where heavy and traditional industries, like iron and steel and vehicle manufacture first developed: many of these are now in decline. The Sunbelt is where new industries are being set up: some of these are traditional industries like furniture making but many of them are modern high-technology industries.

The Manufacturing Belt developed in the last quarter of the nineteenth century. It had a number of locational advantages:

- **Raw materials.** It was rich in natural resources, especially coal, which at the time was industry's main source of energy.
- **Transport.** It had a good system of natural waterways for the transport of raw materials and finished products; for example, iron ore to the west of Lake Superior could be taken by barge through the Great Lakes to the iron and steel towns of Chicago and Pittsburgh (Fig 182).
- **Labour supply.** Most immigrants from Europe arrived at the ports in the north-east of the country, so it was easy for the Manufacturing Belt to recruit large numbers of workers. These, in turn, provided a large market for manufactured goods.

Cities within the Manufacturing Belt tended to specialise in different industries (Fig 183). This stimulated a great deal of trade within the region, which led to the growth of transport and service industries.

Fig 181   Manufacturing industry in the USA: main concentrations

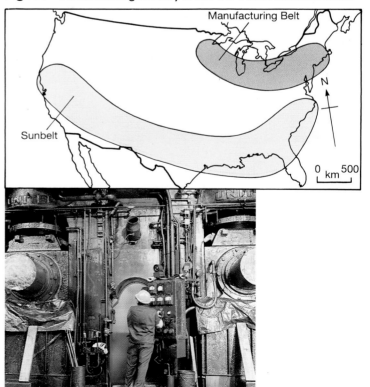

Fig 182   Steel milling, Pittsburgh

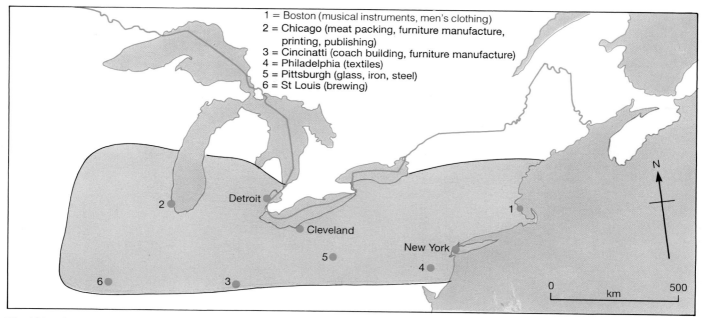

1 = Boston (musical instruments, men's clothing)
2 = Chicago (meat packing, furniture manufacture, printing, publishing)
3 = Cincinatti (coach building, furniture manufacture)
4 = Philadelphia (textiles)
5 = Pittsburgh (glass, iron, steel)
6 = St Louis (brewing)

Fig 183 Specialisation within the Manufacturing Belt

Manufacturing helped to make this region the wealthiest part of the USA. However, it also created problems, particularly for the environment. The Great Lakes were used as a dumping ground for waste products of all kinds and by the 1960s parts of Lake Erie were so badly polluted that it became known as the Dead Sea (Fig 184).

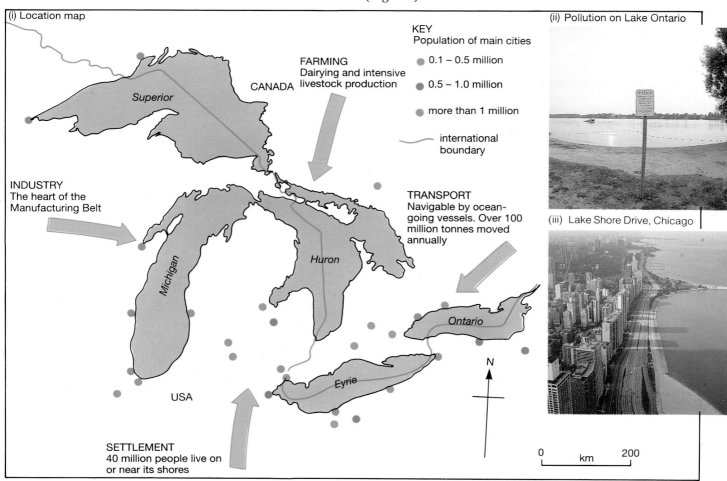

(i) Location map

KEY
Population of main cities
● 0.1 – 0.5 million
● 0.5 – 1.0 million
● more than 1 million
— international boundary

FARMING
Dairying and intensive livestock production

CANADA

INDUSTRY
The heart of the Manufacturing Belt

TRANSPORT
Navigable by ocean-going vessels. Over 100 million tonnes moved annually

Superior

Michigan

Huron

Eyrie

Ontario

USA

SETTLEMENT
40 million people live on or near its shores

(ii) Pollution on Lake Ontario

(iii) Lake Shore Drive, Chicago

0   km   200

Fig 184 Great Lakes: pollution

In 1970 the government passed the Environmental Quality Improvement Act which introduced stricter controls on waste disposal. Other measures followed and these have resulted in some improvement. The decline of heavy industry in recent years has also give the environment a chance to recover.

The decline of traditional manufacturing has affected some parts of the Manufacturing Belt more than others. The north east of the region has suffered the greatest number of job losses because of its reliance on the heavy industries, such as iron and steel, which have been most affected by a fall in demand and an increase in foreign competition. However, the west of the region has actually gained jobs (Fig 185). Overall, it remains one of the wealthiest regions of the country (see Fig 237, page 147).

The growth of manufacturing industry in the Sunbelt has been encouraged by a number of factors. The south and east of the region has benefited from:

● **Raw materials.** Oil and natural gas have led to the development of petroleum refining and chemical manufacture along the Gulf Coast e.g. at Houston (Fig 186).
● **Labour supply.** There has been a big migration of people from the north of the country to the south in search of a warmer climate and a more pleasant environment.
● **Lower wages.** Traditionally, wages have been lower in the southern States. Although this has begun to change in parts of the Sunbelt, it is still true in most of the region; for example, in 1989, in North Carolina, the average wage was 20 per cent below the national average wage.
● **Government influence.** The government has developed the 'space triangle' of Houston, Huntsville and Cape Canaveral (Fig 187) as a centre for the production of military equipment.

Similarly, the west of the region has benefited from an influx of labour; from lower wages; and from the government setting up military factories. However, it has also seen the growth of high-technology industry. Silicon Valley to the south of San Francisco (Fig 188) was the first major area of production: it had a number of locational advantages, including its links with Stanford University and the social and cultural attractions of San Francisco. Production is now more widespread but the main area of concentration is still in California, centred on San Francisco.

	Employment change (millions)
Manufacturing Belt	**2228.1**
New England	−182.6
Mid-Atlantic	−7.1
East North Central	−175.5
West North Central	2410.7
Sunbelt	**6624.0**

Fig 185 Employment change in the USA 1969-1976

Fig 185 shows that the number of manufacturing jobs in the Sunbelt increased by 6.6 million between 1969 and 1976. However, not all parts of the region have benefited from this growth; for example, parts of Texas and Florida have high unemployment rates and there are major areas of deprivation in Los Angeles (see Section 1.4). Indeed, many of the Sunbelt states still rank low in terms of social and economic indicators (see Fig 237, page 147).

Also, some of the Sunbelt's main industries have run into difficulties in recent years. Firstly, the 1980s saw an end to the arms race with the USSR and this has led to the Government cutting back on its orders for military equipment. This, in turn, has led to job losses; for example, in 1990, 30 000 aerospace jobs went in California alone.

Secondly, Silicon Valley has had to face fierce competition from Japan and South Korea, an increase in wages, and tougher environmental laws. As a consequence, some factories have gone out of business completely while others have moved to less expensive parts of the Sunbelt, such as Texas and New Mexico.

Task
1   With the help of an atlas, draw and label a sketch map of the USA to show the following:
   a)   the Manufacturing Belt and the Sunbelt;
   b)   six main towns in each of these regions;
   c)   the types of industry found in each of these regions.
2   Explain why industry developed in the Manufacturing Belt.
3   What advantages and disadvantages has industry brought to the Manufacturing Belt?

Fig 187 Space Launch, Cape Canaveral

Fig 186 Oil refinery, Houston in Texas

Fig 188 Silicon Valley, California, USA

4 Study Fig 189. Describe and explain the relationship, or lack of relationship, between the distribution of energy sources in the USA and **a)** traditional heavy industry and, **b)** modern light and High-technology industry.

5 What has been the main change in the location of manufacturing industry in the USA since 1945 and why has it happened? Use Fig 185 to help you illustrate your answer.

6 To what extent does the distribution of manufacturing industry help to explain the variations in social and economic indicators shown on Fig 237, page 147?

7 What do current trends suggest for the future of manufacturing industry in the USA?

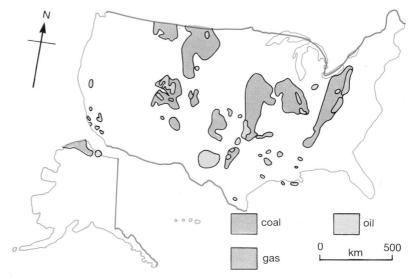

coal   oil

gas   0 km 500

Fig 189 The distribution of energy sources in the USA

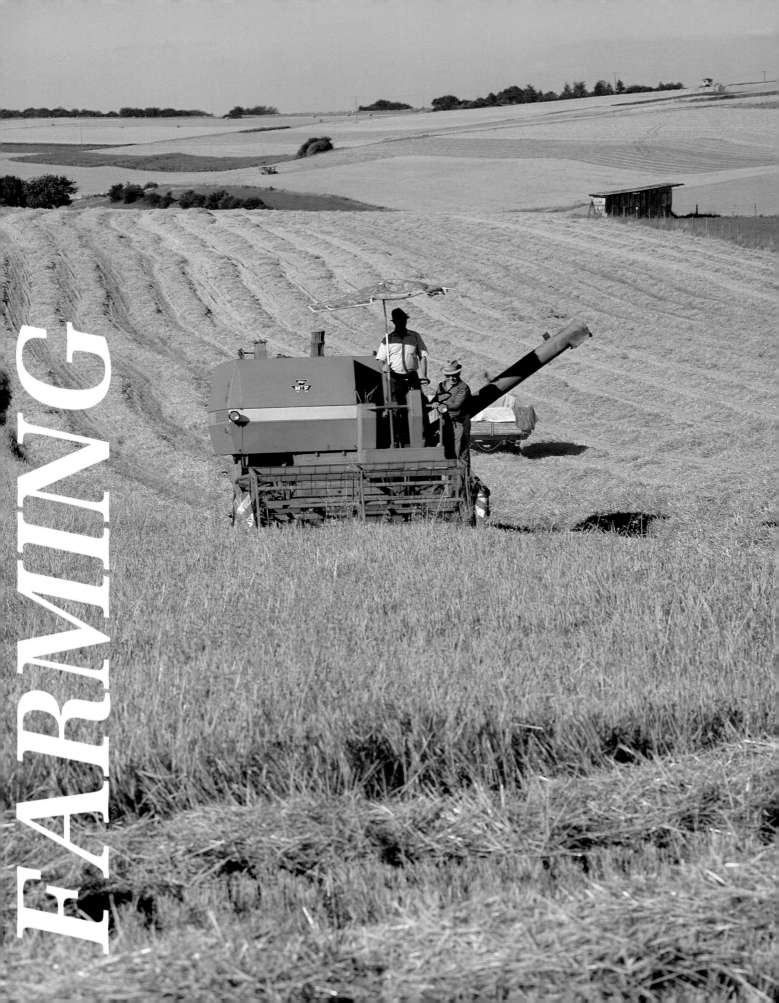

FARMING

4.1 What types of farms are there?

In MEDCs only a small number of people work on farms, although producing food is a very important activity. In LEDCs most people still make their living from farming. There are so many different types of farm worldwide that it is necessary to put them into groups or families.

What do they produce?

A common way of classifying farms is by putting them into groups according to their main product. An **arable farm** specialises in growing crops. A **pastoral farm** specialises in keeping animals. A **mixed farm** grows crops and keeps animals. A **market garden** specialises in growing vegetables, fruit and flowers.

However, farms do not always fit neatly into one group or the other; for example, how many animals does an arable farm have to have before it becomes a mixed farm?

Fig 190   Farm types

What goes in and what comes out?

The things a farm needs to make it work are its **inputs**. What happens on the farm are its **processes**. What it produces are its **outputs**. Fig 191 shows some examples of what is meant by inputs, processes and outputs.

An **intensive farm** is one with high inputs and high outputs per hectare, whereas an **extensive farm** is one with low inputs and low outputs per hectare. Arable farming in East Anglia is intensive (the record yield for a wheat farm in this region is 328 bushels per hectare) while arable farming in the Canadian Prairies is extensive (the average yield is 55 bushels per hectare). However, intensive farms do not always make the most profit because although they produce more the farmer has to spend more money on inputs.

Do they produce food to earn money, or for themselves?

The main aim of a **commercial farm** is to grow food for profit; most farms in MEDCs are of this type. The main aim of a **subsistence farm** is to grow enough food for the family to live on. A few cash crops may be grown which are sold, together with any surplus from the subsistence crops, in order to buy the things which cannot be produced on the farm. Although there are commercial farms in LEDCs – for example, **plantations** – subsistence farms are more common.

Fig 191 Farm inputs and outputs

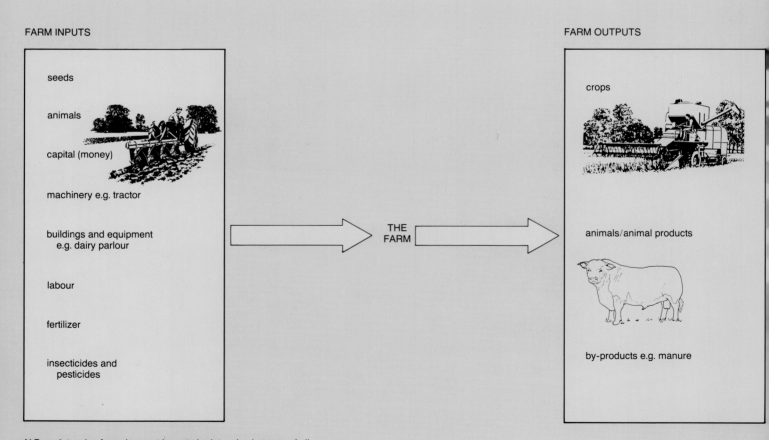

FARM INPUTS

seeds

animals

capital (money)

machinery e.g. tractor

buildings and equipment
    e.g. dairy parlour

labour

fertilizer

insecticides and
    pesticides

THE FARM

FARM OUTPUTS

crops

animals/animal products

by-products e.g. manure

N.B. an intensive farm does not have to be intensive in terms of all of these factors. For example, a farm can be intensive in terms of labour but have very little machinery.

How are they organised?

There are many different ways in which a farm can be organised. Fig 192 compares three of these from the point of view of who owns the land, management and labour.

Are they permanent or temporary?

Most farms are permanent in the sense that the same land is used each year. However, two important types of farming, found mainly in LEDCs, are temporary with different land being used from year to year: **nomadic herding** and **shifting cultivation.**

Nomadic herders move from one place to another as their animals exhaust available pastures and/or water holes; for example, the Masai of East Africa (Fig 193). This is a type of subsistence farming and it requires a large area of land to support even a small number of people.

The shifting cultivator grows crops in a forest clearing for a number of years until the soil loses its fertility (Fig 194). The field is then abandoned and another forest clearing is made by cutting down and burning the vegetation. Again, it is a type of subsistence farming and it can only support low population densities.

Plantation
land ownership – probably owned by a large company
management – run by a manager who is paid a salary by the company
labour – workers live on the plantation in special camps

Share cropping
land ownership – land probably owned by a local landlord
management – the farm is managed by a peasant farmer who pays a share of the crop as rent
labour – the farmer and family

Co-operative
land ownership – the land is probably owned by the farmer
management – the land is managed by the farmer but the co-operative buys and sells on the farmer's behalf
labour – the farmer with paid farm labourers

Fig 192   Farm organisation

Fig 193   Nomadic herders in Kenya

Fig 194 Shifting cultivation, Surinam

ENQUIRY

1 Match the photographs in Fig 190 with the descriptions of the different types of farm according to what they produce.

2 Which of these two farms is intensive and which is extensive? Work out the profit each farm makes and explain the answer you get.

FARM A area = 100 hectares
cost of inputs per hectare
= 10 units
sale price of output per hectare
= 12 units

FARM B area = 200 hectares
cost of inputs per hectare
= 5 units
sale price of output per hectare
= 6 units

3 What do you think is the main difference in the way the farms in Fig 192 are organised?

4 What do you think are some of the advantages and disadvantages of
a) nomadic herding and **b)** shifting cultivation?

4.2 How do farms work?

An arable farm in East Anglia: Low Farm, Buckden

Low Farm covers 200 hectares between the A1 and the River Great Ouse, south and east of the village of Buckden in Cambridgeshire (Figs 195 and 196).

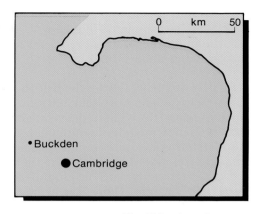

Fig 195 Low Farm, Buckden: location map

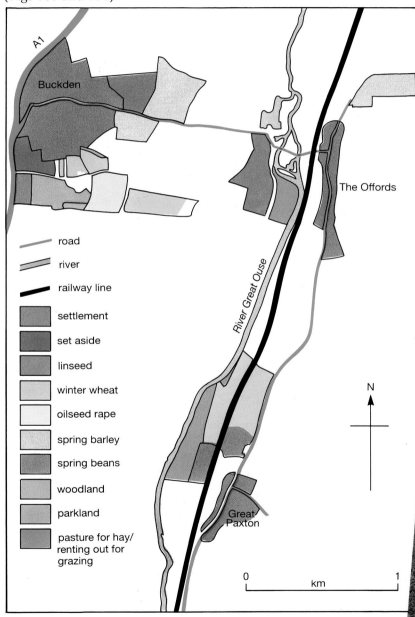

road

river

railway line

settlement

set aside

linseed

winter wheat

oilseed rape

spring barley

spring beans

woodland

parkland

pasture for hay/renting out for grazing

Fig 196 Low Farm, Buckden: land use map

Fig 197 Low Farm

Inputs

The relief of the farm is very flat (Fig 197). The land slopes gently eastwards towards the river. It is well-drained and only the fields next to the river are likely to flood.

Most of the fields have gravel soils which are easy to work and improve, and they help to explain the good drainage. The river meadows are on alluvium (a fine soil deposited by the river) which is very fertile but here, unfortunately, the flood risk stops the farmer from growing arable crops.

Rainfall is relatively low for the British Isles with a yearly average of about 550 mm. It is much the same throughout the year, although there is slightly more in the summer because thunderstorms are quite common. Average temperatures range between 4°C in the winter and 17°C in the summer. The ground is often frozen in the winter. There is an average of six hours bright sunshine a day in the summer and this helps to ripen the crops.

The farm is worked by the landowner and one full-time employee. However, extra labour is provided by the farmer's family at harvest time.

Wheat and barley seed costs on average £37 per hectare. There is a wide variety to choose from. Some types are more resistant to disease than others and they are used for different purposes; for example, most winter barley is grown for animal feed while most spring barley is grown for malting.

Without fertilisers most farms would not make a profit. They are the main reason why yields have gone up; for example, on Low Farm yields per hectare increased by 98 per cent for wheat and 60 per cent for barley between 1954 and 1981. For winter wheat and barley, fertiliser is put on in the autumn when the seeds are sown, and two top dressings are given in the spring; the total cost is £75 per hectare. For spring barley a fertiliser is only put on when the seeds are sown.

Herbicides kill weeds. They are generally used in the autumn and/or the spring. Their cost is on average £20 per hectare. Fungicides kill disease, such as rust, and pesticides kill pests, such as green fly.

Machinery is very important on a modern farm. Low Farm owns a combine harvester which is six years old (Fig 198): new combines are mostly in the £40-50 000 price range although they can cost over £100 000. The farm also has three tractors, a plough, a harrow, a seed drill and a fertiliser spreader. Fuel for these machines costs slightly less than the prices at an ordinary garage.

Buildings include two grain stores, a Dutch barn for hay and straw, a workshop and sheds for machinery.

Fig 198 Combine harvester

Processes

Ploughing turns the soil over and breaks it up in preparation for drilling (Fig 199). This is done in the autumn even if drilling is delayed until the spring.

Harrowing breaks up the clods of earth. The harrow has heavy metal teeth and is pulled along by a tractor.

Drilling is how the seeds are sown. The drill (Fig 200) is drawn along by the tractor and it is designed to feed the seed out at regular intervals and in straight rows. Winter wheat and barley are sown in the autumn and germinate before the frosts and cold weather stop plant growth over the winter. Other crops are sown in the spring.

Spraying and top dressing of fertiliser is done at any time between autumn and mid-summer according to the weather and the stage the crop has reached.

Haymaking is generally done in June or July. This work is contracted out because the farm does not own the specialist machinery required for this job.

The crops ripen at different times but most of the harvesting is done in June, July and August.

Storage and quality control are two very important processes. The grain may be stored for several months before it is sold and it has to be dried thoroughly and checked daily.

General farm maintenance includes cutting the hedgerows each year, maintaining ditches and drains, looking after areas of woodland and overhauling machinery.

Different crops take out different sorts and amounts of goodness from the soil. If you grow the same crop in the same field year after year the soil becomes exhausted. However, if you rotate the crops the soil has a chance to recover. On Low Farm, linseed and oilseed rape are grown in different fields each year so that all fields have a break from cereals every fourth or fifth year.

Fig 199 Ploughing

Outputs

The farm's outputs are, of course, its crops. Some examples of prices are: winter wheat £120 a tonne; winter barley £100 a tonne; spring barley £140 a tonne; hay £60 a tonne. The grain is sold to a local grain merchant over a period of time.

Also, the farmer gets **area payments** from the government for growing certain crops, and for **set aside** (the land he has agreed not to grow any crops on); these points are explained in more detail in Section 4.3.

ENQUIRY

1 Draw an inputs/processes/outputs diagram to show how Low Farm works.
2 What are the river meadows used for, and why?
3 What do you notice about where the fields are on Low Farm? What problems does this cause the farmer?
4 Work out the cost of seed, fertiliser and two applications of herbicide per hectare for winter wheat. If average yield is six tonnes per hectare what price does the farmer get? What is the difference between the two figures?
5 Your answer to question four is, of course, very different to the amount of profit the farmer makes. Make a list of all the things you can think of that the farmer has to pay for to keep the farm working.

Fig 200 A seed drill

A subsistence farm in Kenya

This farm is at Kabare which is 60 km south of Mount Kenya (Fig 201). It covers about five acres which is the average size of a subsistence farm in this region. It supports a family of 12, although two have part-time jobs elsewhere; one in the local coffee factory and one as a home-help for the family of a local college lecturer.

About three acres of the farm is used for growing the two staple crops of maize and beans (Fig 203). They are grown in the same field – one row of maize, then one of beans, and so on. The bean pods are left to dry on the plant before they are harvested, about three months after sowing. The maize takes longer to ripen. Some is picked and eaten as corn on the cob while the rest is left to dry and then ground into maize flour.

About two acres is used to grow coffee as a cash crop. This is enough room for several hundred coffee bushes (Fig 202). The soil at Kabare is naturally fertile but the farmers who can afford to use fertiliser get a better crop. When the coffee beans have been harvested they are taken to the local coffee co-operative factory. The beans are graded for quality and the number of kilos each farmer brings is recorded. About three or four times a year there is 'coffee money' when people go to the factory to collect the money their coffee has earnt. This money is used to buy the things they are unable to produce on the farm and to pay for expenses such as medical bills and school fees.

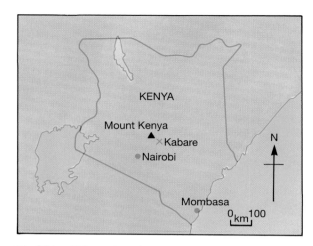

Fig 201   Kabare: location map

Fig 202   Picking coffee

Fig 203   Maize field

Many other crops are grown in small quantities on the farm such as tomatoes, potatoes, chilli peppers and aubergines. There is usually a cow for milk, a few goats and a fair number of chickens for eggs and meat.

There are two rainy seasons – the long rains from April until June and the short rains from mid-October until early December. Planting is carried out at the start of each rainy season so two crops are usually possible.

The tools used on the farm are very simple. The 'panga' is a broad heavy knife with a wooden handle (Fig 204). It is used for practically everything – for example, preparing the soil, digging holes for planting and cutting down or digging up weeds. The 'jembe' has three metal prongs (Fig 205); it is used for hoeing and raking the soil and for digging up potatoes. Threshing the beans from their pods is done by beating them on a sheet of plastic with large sticks. The beans settle to the bottom and the dried pods can then be removed from on top and used instead of firewood as they make a very good fuel.

Fig 204 Cutting cocoa pods with a panga

ENQUIRY

1 Draw an inputs-processes-outputs diagram for this farm.
2 What is meant by a staple crop?
3 Why is the coffee crop so important to this farm?
4 How does farming at Kabare depend on the seasons?
5 Do you think machinery would help this farm? Explain your answer.

Fig 205 Jembe tool

4.3 Agriculture in the European Union – what it is like, and why?

The pattern of agriculture in the EU

Fig 206 shows the distribution of the main types of farming in the EU. Although it gives less information than a map of an individual country (for example Fig 208, page 130), it allows broad patterns to be identified.

Different regions of the EU specialise in particular crops. For example, the market gardens of northern Europe grow potatoes, apples and tulips whereas in southern Europe they grow olives, oranges and grapes. There are differences in livestock production as well: the UK is a leading producer of sheep meat whereas Greece is a leading producer of goat meat.

Many factors have contributed to the pattern of agriculture in the EU today. The following Enquiry concentrates on the physical influences on farming, and the political, economic and technological influences are considered in the case studies which follow.

Fig 206   The pattern of agriculture in the EU

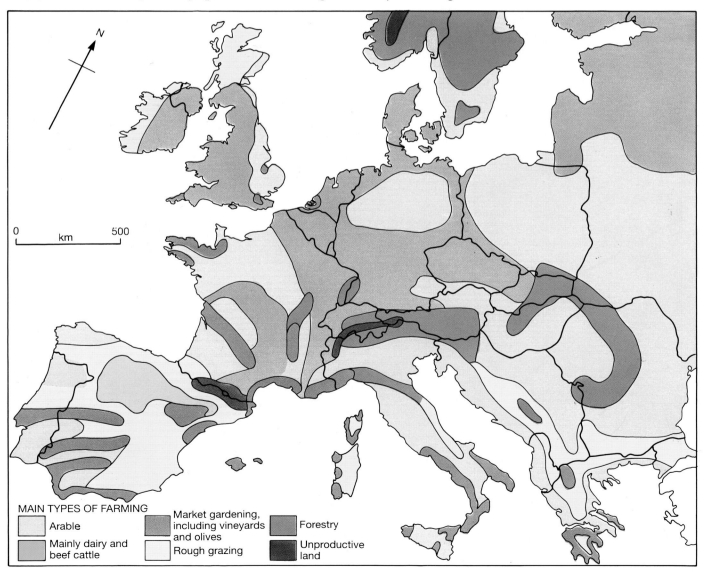

MAIN TYPES OF FARMING

- Arable
- Mainly dairy and beef cattle
- Market gardening, including vineyards and olives
- Rough grazing
- Forestry
- Unproductive land

1 Compare the distribution of arable farming with that of dairy and beef farming. Which is found more in the east of the EU and which is found more in the west? What relationship is there between this pattern and Europe's climate? (Find out about temperature and rainfall from an atlas.)

2 What relationship is there between the distribution of rough grazing, forestry and unproductive land on the one hand, and relief and climate on the other?

3 Use Fig 207 to help you to explain why the market gardens of northern and southern Europe specialise in growing different crops.

4 Compare the distribution of market gardening in Spain and Portugal with a map showing the main rivers of this part of Europe. What is the relationship and what might explain it?

Farming in the UK

Fig 208 shows the distribution of the main types of farm in the British Isles. Compare this map with maps in an atlas showing relief, rainfall, winter and summer temperatures, soils, towns, cities and main road and rail links. Then complete the next Enquiry.

potatoes
temperatures above freezing but below 21°C; good summer rainfall or irrigation

carrots
temperatures between 15°C and 20°C; moderate summer rainfall

apples
long, sunny summer days; 500 mm – 1000 mm rain per year

oranges
average summer temperatures between 20°C and 25°C; good rainfall or irrigation

olives
average summer temperatures greater than 18°C; 400 mm–900 mm of rain a year but dry autumns

grapes
average summer temperatures 18°C to 22°C; good water supply in spring but dry summers

Fig 207 Crop requirements

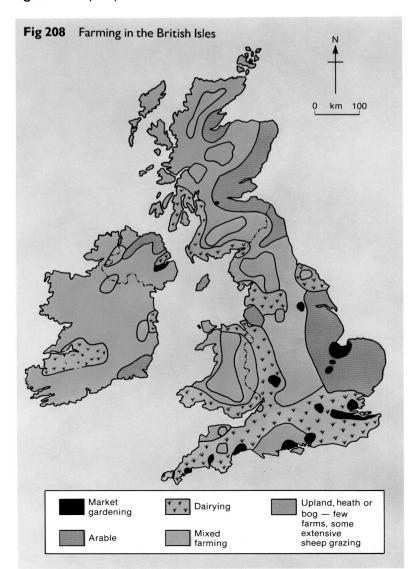

Fig 208 Farming in the British Isles

N

0 km 100

Legend:
- ■ Market gardening
- Arable
- ⌄⌄ Dairying
- Mixed farming
- Upland, heath or bog — few farms, some extensive sheep grazing

	Mild winters, early springs	Hot, sunny summers	Drier climate	Wetter climate	Mountainous relief	Fertile soils	Near to large cities	Good road/rail links to large cities
market gardening								
arable								
dairying								
extensive grazing (sheep)								
mixed farming								

Fig 209 Farm factors table

ENQUIRY

1   Complete a copy of Fig 209 by writing a comment about each of the factors for each of the types of farm.
2   Describe and explain the distribution of each of the main types of farm in the British Isles. Use Fig 208 for your description and include the following key words/phrases; north; south; east; west; central; upland; hilly; lowland; towns; cities; main road and rail links. Your explanation should make use of the information you gathered for Fig 209, and it should also include these extra points:
  • grass will not grow if temperatures fall below 6°C;
  • grass grows best in areas of moderate rainfall;
  • steep slopes have poor, thin soils;
  • it is difficult to use machinery on steep slopes;
  • mountainous regions are exposed to bad weather;
  • arable crops need dry, sunny weather for ripening.

Before 1940 nearly 70 per cent of the UK's food was imported and this led to shortages during the Second World War. Consequently, the government decided to encourage food production. It set a guaranteed price for farm produce and, because farmers could be certain of selling everything, they began to look for ways of increasing output. This kind of help continued when the UK joined the EU in 1973.

Many changes have taken place. There has been a big increase in the amount of machinery used and a big decrease in the number of farm workers (Fig 210). In the arable regions thousands of kilometres of hedgerows have been uprooted to make bigger fields so that it is easier to make efficient use of this machinery. However it has destroyed the habitat of many plants and animals and it has completely changed the look of the landscape from one of small enclosed fields to one of large open fields.

Year	Tractors	Combines	Farm workers (full-time)	Horses
1940	100	10	660	550
1950	290	20	620	270
1960	430	50	490	60
1970	480	70	300	20
1980	490	60	190	0
1985	490	50	160	0

Fig 210   The effects of mechanisation, figures in '000s

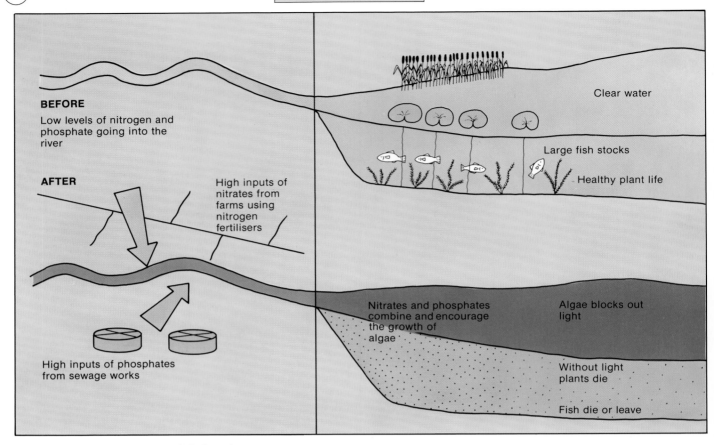

BEFORE

Low levels of nitrogen and phosphate going into the river

AFTER

High inputs of nitrates from farms using nitrogen fertilisers

High inputs of phosphates from sewage works

Clear water

Large fish stocks

Healthy plant life

Nitrates and phosphates combine and encourage the growth of algae

Algae blocks out light

Without light plants die

Fish die or leave

Fig 211   Pollution on the Norfolk Broads

There has been a big increase in the use of chemical fertilisers, pesticides, fungicides and herbicides: the use of nitrogen fertilisers increased from 210 000 tonnes in 1950 to 1 470 000 tonnes in 1983. During the same period the average yield of grain crops doubled.

However there has been a growing concern about the impact of these chemical inputs. Nitrogen fertilisers are washed into streams and rivers and find their way into underground water supplies. Fig 211 shows how a combination of nitrogen and phosphate has led to the death of large parts of the Norfolk Broads.

Fig 212 is an attractive reminder of what fields used to look like before the days of regular spraying. The farmer was unable to treat this field of barley because of wet weather, and the result was this brilliant display of poppies. The number of poppies is relatively small and will not seriously affect the crop.

New crops have been introduced. The EU, in order to cut imports of vegetable oil, has encouraged farmers to grow oilseed rape by paying them subsidies. Between 1973 and 1986 the amount grown increased from 8000 to 280 000 hectares and the rape's distinctive yellow flowers have added a new colour to the May countryside (Fig 213). More recently, linseed has been encouraged with subsidies of £250 per acre. It is used to make linoleum and industrial oil (Fig 214).

Pastoral farming has also seen many developments. Artificial insemination has made it much easier to control breeding and as a result there has been a rapid improvement in the quality of stock. New drugs have helped to control disease and animals reared for meat can be injected with hormones to increase their growth rate. Silage has replaced hay as the main winter fodder because it has a higher feed value. These changes increased livestock production in the UK by 50 per cent between 1954 and 1981.

However, not everyone thinks that these developments are for the best. Concern has been expressed about the use of certain drugs and hormones because of their possible effect on us when we eat the products. Silage has to be prepared carefully because if it gets too wet it produces an effluent which can kill river life completely.

Fig 212 Poppy field

Fig 213 Oilseed rape

Fig 214 Linseed

Factory farming, especially of chickens and pigs, has become widespread. Nine out of ten laying hens and eight out of ten chickens bred for cooking are kept in 'batteries'. The batteries are large sheds (Fig 215) in which conditions are carefully controlled. The laying hens are placed in individual cages when they are 16 to 20 weeks old. They automatically receive a fixed amount of food and water each day. Their first laying cycle lasts 32 weeks. Rather than wait for their next cycle to begin they are sent for slaughter. Chickens bred especially for cooking are fattened up and sold after eight weeks. None of these birds see the light of day until they leave the battery for slaughter.

Free range poultry (Fig 216) need more space and they 'waste' some of the energy they get from their food, in moving around. Their eggs are more difficult to collect. Consequently, free range eggs and chickens are more expensive than battery ones.

The number of farms has fallen from 450 000 to 300 000, mainly because small farms have been taken over by large farms; it is increasingly difficult for the small farm to afford the expensive machinery and other inputs which are needed to make a profit. More and more farms are owned by companies and are run as **agribusinesses** rather than being owned by an independent farmer.

Overall, agricultural production has increased by over 50 per cent since 1945 and the percentage of food imported has fallen to 50 per cent. So, although there are problems and concerns, the aim of increasing food production has been achieved.

ENQUIRY

1 Draw a composite line graph to show the statistics in Fig 210. Describe and explain the changes your graph shows. What impact have these changes had on the farm landscape?

2 What is your own reaction to the landscapes shown in Figures 212, 213 and 214? Say whether or not you like the landscapes and what you think of the issues behind the photographs. Do you think farmers should use less herbicide? What are the advantages and disadvantages of reducing imported oils such as soya beans, cottonseed and groundnuts from, mainly, EDCs? Should farmers be paid £250 an acre for growing linseed when the crop itself is only worth £90 an acre?

3 What are the arguments for and against intensive stock production?

4 Find out the difference in price between free range and battery eggs. Do you think battery hen houses should be allowed? Explain your point of view.

5 Overall, do you think the changes in UK farming in the last 50 years have been for the better or for the worse? Explain your point of view.

Fig 215 Battery hen house

Fig 216 Free range hens

Farming in Denmark

Farming is extremely important to the Danish economy. It employs five per cent of the workforce, provides the raw materials for its food processing industry and accounts for nearly 30 per cent of the total value of its exports.

Physical factors – particularly soils and climate – have an important influence on farming in Denmark. Soils are of two main types. During the Ice Age an ice sheet covered the eastern half of the country. As the ice melted streams flowing out from this ice sheet deposited infertile sands and gravels over much of the western half. Over the eastern half the melting ice deposited a layer of more fertile boulder clay. Farms are larger on the less fertile sands and gravels than they are on the more fertile boulder clays because they are less productive (Fig 217).

Rainfall is evenly distributed throughout the year and averages about 50 mm a month. Denmark has warm summers which allow arable crops to ripen but temperatures are too low for grass to grow for several months during the winter. This helps to explain why much of the land is used to grow arable crops for fodder but only eight per cent of the land is given over to permanent pasture.

Economic factors are also important in explaining the type of farming found in Denmark. In fact, before the last quarter of the nineteenth century arable farming was the major activity. However, Danish farmers found that they were unable to compete with the arable farms of the Prairies in North America and the Steppes in Russia which began producing grain for the world market at this time. It was only by switching to pastoral farming that they managed to stay in business.

Fig 218 A dairy farm in Denmark

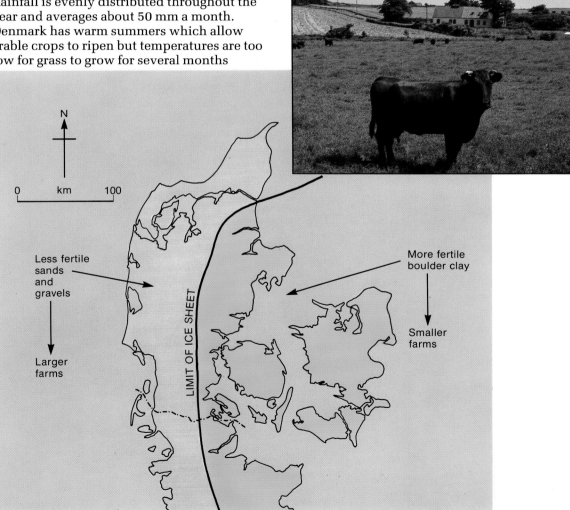

Fig 217 Soils in Denmark

Pastoral farming – cattle and pigs – is the most important type of farming in Denmark. Dairy farming is more concentrated in the west of the country where the less fertile soils have been improved for pasture, oats and potatoes (Fig 218). Pig farming is more concentrated in the east which is also the main region for arable farming.

However, Fig 219 shows that there have been big changes in the type of farming in the last 25 years. Keeping cattle and pigs together used to be the norm rather than the exception: the pigs were fed on the skimmed milk and whey which are by-products of butter production. The increase in specialisation has come about because of the need to be more efficient in the face of tougher competition.

The increase in arable farming is the other notable trend in Fig 219. This has happened because of the fall in the demand for dairy produce, and because of the Common Agricultural Policy (**CAP**) which has cut subsidies on dairy produce in order to reduce over-production.

Another change has been a trend towards larger farm holdings, although the majority of farms in Denmark are still relatively small and family-run (Fig 220). As such, the success of Danish farming still depends to a large extent on the way its small farms have organised themselves into **co-operatives**.

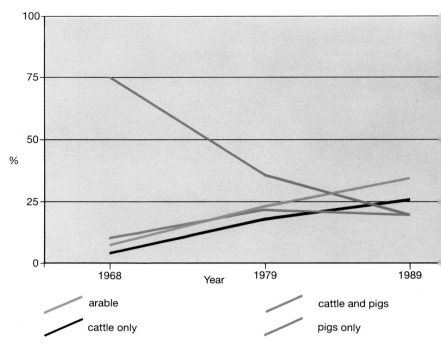

Fig 219 Changes in Danish farming

On average about 400 farms make up a single co-operative. It arranges many things which a small farm would be unable to do on its own. It can bulk-buy seed and fertiliser which cuts costs. It can negotiate cheaper loans with the banks because of the combined spending power of its individual farms. Each farm can

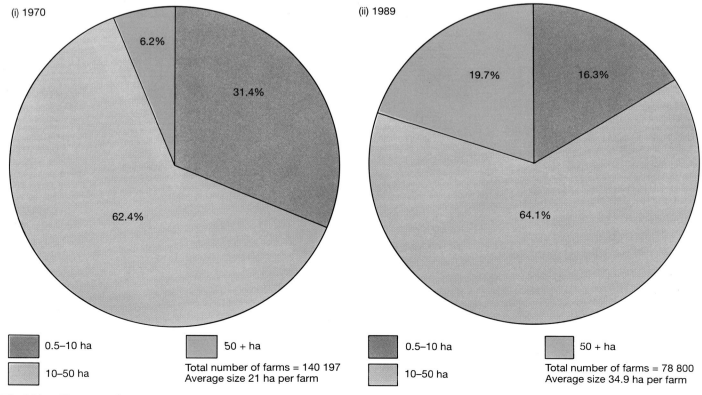

Fig 220 Changes in farm size

contribute towards the cost of expensive machinery which the co-operative can buy and loan out on a rota basis. The co-operative can organise large-scale advertising and marketing. All savings and profits are, of course, passed back to the farms.

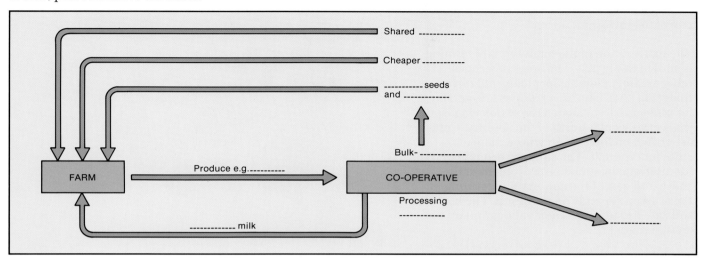

Fig 221   The advantages of a co-operative

Denmark joined the EU in 1973 at the same time as the UK and Ireland for these two main reasons: the UK was its main trading partner for agricultural produce; and it wanted to benefit from the price levels being charged by the rest of the EU. Membership has affected its trading pattern, with a decline in exports to the UK but an increase in exports to other EU countries. It has also found new markets in Japan, USA and the Middle East (Fig 222).

1   How have **a)** physical and **b)** economic factors affected the character and type of farming in Denmark?
2   Describe and explain the trends shown in Fig 219.
3   Make a copy of Fig 221. Complete it by using the words in the following list: machinery; skimmed; loans; fertiliser; factory; marketing; buying; cheaper; marketing; milk.
4   Can you think of any disadvantages of sharing machinery on a rota basis?
5   How has farming in Denmark been affected by its membership of the EU?

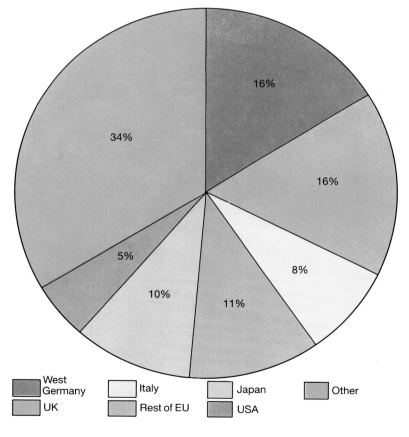

Fig 222   The destination of Denmark's agricultural exports

Farming in Spain

Farming is an important sector of the Spanish economy. It employs 12 per cent of its population, accounts for six per cent of its GDP and 15 per cent of its exports. However, its overall level of productivity per person is one of the lowest in Europe.

The distribution of the main types of farming is shown in Fig 223. The areas of steepest relief are only suitable for sheep and olive trees (Fig 224). The lower slopes are suitable for vineyards. The main area of dairying is in the wetter, cooler north of the country. Cereals are grown on lower land where there is sufficient rainfall. The summer drought of the Mediterranean climate is a problem in the south and east of the country and farming in these areas depends on irrigation. The best soils are found in the river valleys and on the coastal plain.

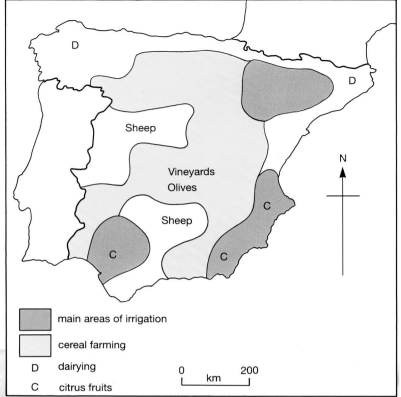

Fig 223　Distribution of farming in Spain

Fig 224　Sheep grazing in Andalucia

Farming has been hampered in the past by inefficient systems of land ownership and by old-fashioned methods. In the north the problem has been **minifundia** – small-scale subsistence farms with scattered fields and a heavy reliance on animals rather than machines. In the centre and south the problem has been **latifundia** – large estates given over to the extensive cultivation of cereals, often owned by absentee landlords (who do not live on the farm and who do not take a close interest in its operation), and worked by cheap peasant labour.

However, this picture is beginning to change. A great deal of marginal land has been taken out of production and the area farmed fell from 3 million hectares in 1962 to 1.8 million hectares in 1987. There has been a big decrease in the number of people employed in farming (37 per cent between 1975 and 1985). Minifundia have been consolidated to make larger, more economic farms; for example, the average size of farm increased from 14 hectares in 1962 to 19 hectares in 1982. This figure would be greater but it includes the break-up of latifundia into smaller units, and the development of small market gardens (see below).

The major change, though, has been the increase in the amount of irrigated land which went up from 2.4 million hectares in 1972 to 3.1 million hectares in 1988. This has been accompanied by the introduction of modern, capital-intensive production of fruit, vegetables and flowers for export.

Generally, rivers have been dammed and water is taken in channels to small fields called **huertas** (Fig 225). However, in Almeira province huge underground sources of water have been tapped which supply 15 000 market gardens. Much of the area is covered with plastic greenhouses and the average size of the farms is only 0.75 hectares. However, productivity is very high and in 1986 over 200 000 tonnes was exported.

In 1986 Spain became a member of the EU. Its market gardens should benefit as tariffs are reduced on its exports to other EU countries. It should also benefit from policies designed to help 'Mediterranean' crops (for example, reducing the level of support for arable crops which are grown mainly in the temperate north); and from policies designed to help the poorer regions of the community (for example, help given to 'less-favoured areas' – see Fig 228, page 141). Consequently, the

improvements described above should continue into the foreseeable future.

ENQUIRY

1 With the help of an atlas, and the information in this section, describe and explain the distribution of the different types of farming in Spain. In your answer, deal with physical and human factors under separate headings.
2 Describe the main differences between the types of farming shown in Figs 224 and 225.
3 Explain what is meant by minifundia and latifundia. Why are these systems of land ownership inefficient?
4 Give three reasons why productivity per worker in Spain increased by 35 per cent between 1980 and 1990.
5 Describe and explain the major change which has affected Spanish farming in recent years.
6 How are the changes in Spanish farming being helped by its membership of the EU?

Fig 225   Huerta in Malaga

The EU and farming

The EU controls farming through its Common Agricultural Policy (CAP) and some of the ways in which it has influenced the development of agriculture have already been mentioned in the sections about the UK, Denmark and Spain.

The CAP was set up at a time when food was in short supply and one of its main aims was to encourage production. It did this by setting a guaranteed price: if the farmer received less than this the Union made up the difference.

This policy was successful because, with the certainty of a good price, farmers grew as much as they could. By the 1980s the food shortage had turned into a food surplus and the EU was having to store large amounts of produce (Fig 226). The cost of this was rising all the time (Fig 227) and it was the cause of many arguments between member countries. On several occasions it came close to breaking up the Union.

Another way in which the CAP has influenced farming is through its 'less-favoured' areas policy. Regions where farming is difficult and/or in need of modernisation have been identified (Fig 228) and they have been given special help such as extra **subsidies**, money for new equipment and support for special projects. For example, hill farmers have been given grants for new machinery as long as they share it between at least three farms, known as a 'forage group'.

Fig 226 Grain store

Cost of surpluses

AGRICULTURE

By Rosemary Collins

THE cost of buying and storing surplus food has pushed up estimates of next year's agricultural budget by £90 million to £2,550 million.

Common Market farm price support systems are now expected to cost double the domestic agriculture budget, at £1,660 million compared to £880 million, in 1987-88. The main surpluses in the UK are of wheat, butter, skimmed milk powder and, to a much lesser extent, beef.

The UK taxpayer bears the cost of buying and storing such food and pockets the proceeds from any eventual sale with the EEC making good the shortfall between the guaranteed purchase price and the selling price, and paying export subsidies in certain cases.

The latest estimate compares with projected total agricultural expenditure of £2,117 million in the current financial year, £1,481 million of which is reckoned to be going on Common Market price support buying.

Fig 227 Cost of surpluses

More recently, there have been attempts to produce 'Integrated Operations' which involve pulling together all the different types of help the Union gives. For example, the Integrated Mediterranean Programme was approved in 1985 with the aim of modernising industry as well as agriculture in the poorer regions of the south.

The EU's trade policy has also influenced farming. The overall effect of subsidies has been to protect the European farmer from cheap imports and this situation has been maintained by agreements such as the Lome Convention and **GATT** (see Section 6.3).

Fig 228 Less-favoured areas

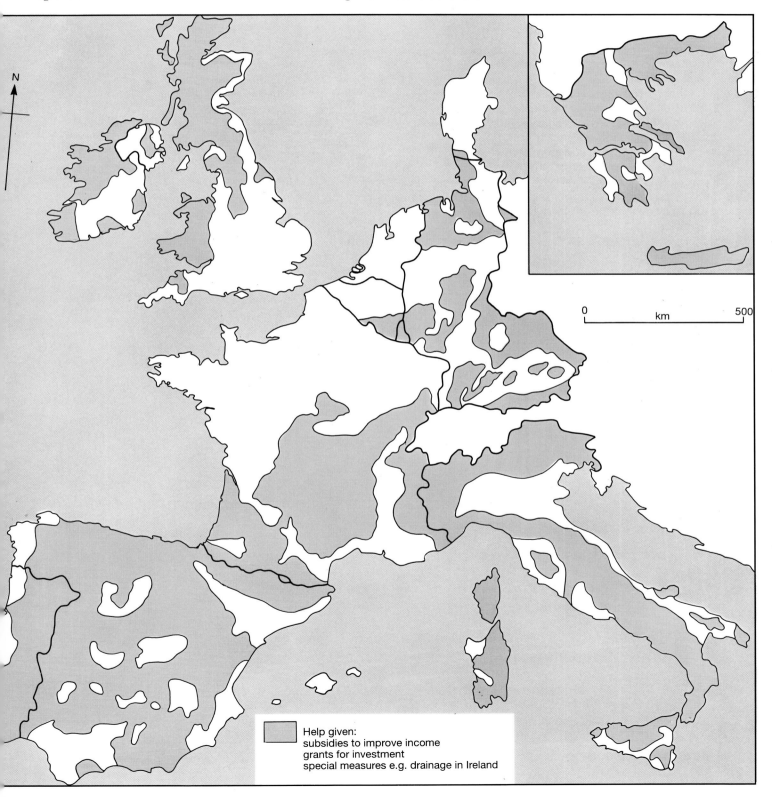

Help given:
subsidies to improve income
grants for investment
special measures e.g. drainage in Ireland

The most effective – and expensive – part of the CAP has been its system of **guaranteed prices**. Concern about the food and drink surpluses, the cost of the policy (in the 1980s it accounted for 70 per cent of the community's budget) and the threat of trade barriers being put up by non-EU countries led to the reform of the CAP in 1992.

For arable crops, guaranteed prices are being phased out. They are being replaced by 'area payments' – money given for growing certain crops per acre – which will also be gradually reduced. However, farmers only get these payments if they agree to 'set aside' – not grow food crops on – 15 per cent of their land each year for five years. An area payment is given for set aside as well; in other words, farmers are being paid not to grow food. They are allowed to use the land for activities such as caravan and camping sites, riding schools and golf courses, and this is leading to a change from farming to other types of land use (Fig 229).

Fig 229 Lakeside Lodge Golf Club, Cambridgeshire

The policies to do with pastoral farming have also been reformed. The guaranteed price for beef has been cut, and the number of animals allowed per acre is being reduced. Also, farmers are being encouraged to keep animals on the farm for longer by giving them a special payment called the **beef premium** in two instalments – the first when the animal is ten months old and the second when it is 23 months old.

The milk **quota** – the amount of milk which a farmer is allowed to produce – is being cut and the farmers will be paid compensation at the rate of four pence per litre for the next ten years. The guaranteed price for butter is being reduced.

There have, as yet, been no major changes to the regulations which control sheep farming. Therefore, for example, the limit on the number of animals a farmer is allowed to keep remains in force at 4.6 per hectare.

It is too early to predict with certainty what the effect of these new policies will be. Set aside may not, in fact, reduce production because farmers do not have to take their best land out of cultivation. However, arable farmers know that, as subsidies are reduced, they are going to face greater competition on the world market; some ways in which they could adjust to this situation are shown in Fig 230. Demand for beef is still high but a reduction in dairying, as in Denmark, seems likely to continue.

- Join together to form larger farms; it is cheaper per acre to farm 1000 acres than 100 acres.

- Increase the normal working life of machinery by carrying out more repairs.

- Introduce more crop rotations to increase fertility, rather than spend money on chemical fertilisers.

- Concentrate on crops which people want to buy, rather than crops which produce the greatest yield.

- Cut down on chemical inputs by spraying for diseases as they appear, rather than spraying for overall prevention.

Fig 230 Adjusting to the world market

4.4 **Assessment task:** *Farming in the EU*

Design an A3 sized poster which includes the following:

a) A clearly labelled map to show and explain the distribution of the main types of farm in either the UK, Denmark or Spain.

b) A diagram to show how and why farming in one region of your chosen country has changed in the last 50 years.

c) A short account to explain how the Common Agricultural Policy has influenced farming in the EU, and what its main consequences have been.

d) A table to show the possible implications of Fig 230 for **i)** how arable farms are organised and run **ii)** consumers and **iii)** the environment.

e) A short account to explain which of the following policies you think will make European agriculture **i)** more competitive and **ii)** less competitive on the world market: guaranteed prices; area payments; set aside; the beef premium; and milk quotas.

DEVELOPMENT

5.1 What do we mean by development?

In 1980 a group of experts published a report called 'North-South: A Programme For Survival'. They separated the world's MEDCs from its LEDCs with a **development line** (Fig 231). Their Chairperson, Willy Brandt, who used to be Chancellor of West Germany, said that this line represented "*a gap so wide that at the extremes people seem to live in different worlds*".

However, defining development can be difficult; for example, people have different ideas about what a developed country should be like. Measuring development is also difficult; for example there is not a statistic called 'development' so it is necessary to collect facts (called indicators) which give an idea of how developed a country is. Some of these problems are explored in the following Enquiry.

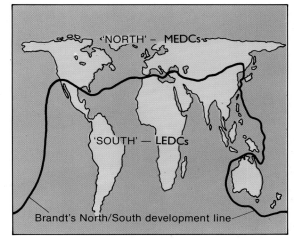

Fig 231 North and South

ENQUIRY

1 Study the development indicators in Fig 232. Choose the ten which you think are the best. Put them in rank order with the one which you think is most important first. Compare your list with those of others in your class. Did you choose the same indicators? Discuss why there were differences between your lists.

2 The indicators in Fig 232 are of two different types: economic (to do with money); and social (to do with people). Which of the three lists is made up of: **a)** only economic indicators; **b)** only social indicators; and **c)** a mixture of economic and social indicators?

3 Which of these lists do you think gives the best overall picture of development, and why?

4 Which of the indicators do you think would be particularly difficult to get statistics for?

5 Think over your answers to the above questions. What are some of the reasons that explain why it is difficult to define and measure development?

LIST A
- per cent of children given free state education;
- number of people per doctor;
- birth rate;
- child death rate;
- per cent of adults who can read.

LIST B
- average wage;
- energy (amount used per person);
- per cent of people employed in manufacturing industry;
- unemployment rate;
- value of exports and imports.

LIST C
- press freedom (how free newspapers are to print what they want);
- status of women (e.g. are they allowed to vote?);
- industrial production;
- road density (amount of road per km^2);
- number of political prisoners.

Fig 232 Development indicators

The world pattern of development

ENQUIRY

1 Make a copy of Fig 234. Complete it by using the statistics in Fig 235 and the scoring system (Fig 233). The first country has been done for you.

2 Add up the total score for each country. (If a country has a blank because one of the statistics is unavailable do not give it an overall total.)

3 On a world map outline mark on and label **a)** Brandt's 'North-South development line'; and **b)** the boundaries of the 25 countries in Fig 235.

4 Add the key shown in Fig 236 to the map and use it to shade in the countries according to their total score.

5 Does your map show a North-South development gap?

6 Does your map show variations within the northern region?

7 Does your map show variations within the southern region?

8 What problems with measuring development did you come across in carrying out this exercise?

Infant mortality		Food supply	
Value	Score	Value	Score
60+	1	3000+	4
40-59	2	2500-2999	3
20-39	3	2000-2499	2
0-19	4	1500-1999	1

Telephones		GNP	
Value	Score	Value	Score
40+	4	6000+	4
20-39	3	4000-5999	3
10-19	2	2000-3999	2
0-9	1	0-1999	1

Fig 233 Scoring system

		Infant mortality	Food supply	Telephones	GNP	Total Score
1	Argentina	3	4	2	2	11
2	Australia					
3	Bangladesh					
4	Brazil					
5	Canada					
6	China					
7	CIS					
8	Ecuador					
9	Egypt					
10	France					
11	Hong Kong					
12	India					
13	Italy					
14	Jamaica					
15	Japan					
16	Kenya					
17	Libya					
18	New Zealand					
19	Nigeria					
20	Philippines					
21	Saudi Arabia					
22	Spain					
23	UK					
24	USA					
25	Venezuela					

Fig 234 Score chart

Contrasts within countries

As well as variations in the level of development between MEDCs and LEDCs, variations within MEDCs and LEDCs are found. So, although Fig 235 draws attention to the differences between the USA and Brazil, Figs 237 and 238 show that some parts of these countries are better off than others.

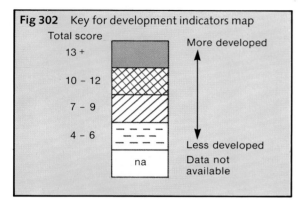

Fig 302 Key for development indicators map

Total score

13 + — More developed

10 – 12

7 – 9

4 – 6

na — Less developed

na — Data not available

Fig 236 Key for development indicators map

		Infant mortality	Food supply	Telephones	GNP
1	Argentina	29	3168	11.6	2160
2	Australia	9	3347	63.0	14 440
3	Bangladesh	108	1925	0.08	180
4	Brazil	57	2703	9.0	2550
5	Canada	7	3451	78.0	19 020
6	China	27	2637	0.7	360
7	CIS	20	3382	13.0	3800
8	Ecuador	57	2302	4.0	1040
9	Egypt	57	3196	3.0	630
10	France	7	3312	66.0	17 830
11	Hong Kong	6	2883	47.0	10 320
12	India	88	2104	0.6	350
13	Italy	9	3571	48.8	15 150
14	Jamaica	14	2579	n/a	1260
15	Japan	5	2822	62.0	23 730
16	Kenya	64	2016	1.4	380
17	Libya	68	3393	n/a	6000
18	New Zealand	9	3476	69.7	11 800
19	Nigeria	96	2083	0.4	250
20	Philippines	40	2238	1.7	700
21	Saudi Arabia	58	2805	18.0	6230
22	Spain	9	3494	39.6	9150
23	UK	8	3259	60.0	14 570
24	USA	8	3644	70.0	21 100
25	Venezuela	33	2534	9.2	2450

Infant mortality = the number of babies who die before the age of one per 1000 live births
Food supply = calories per person per day (the average requirement is 2400)
Telephones = the number of telephones per 100 people
GNP = US $ per capita
n/a = data not available

Fig 235 Development indicators for selected countries

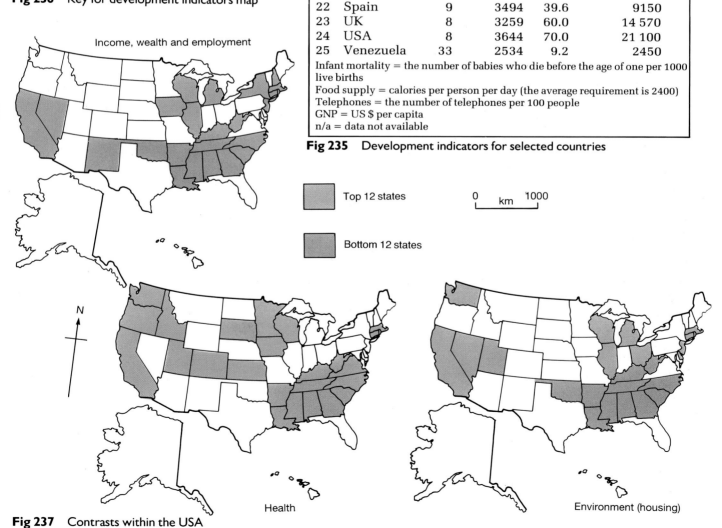

Income, wealth and employment

Top 12 states

Bottom 12 states

0 km 1000

N

Health

Environment (housing)

Fig 237 Contrasts within the USA

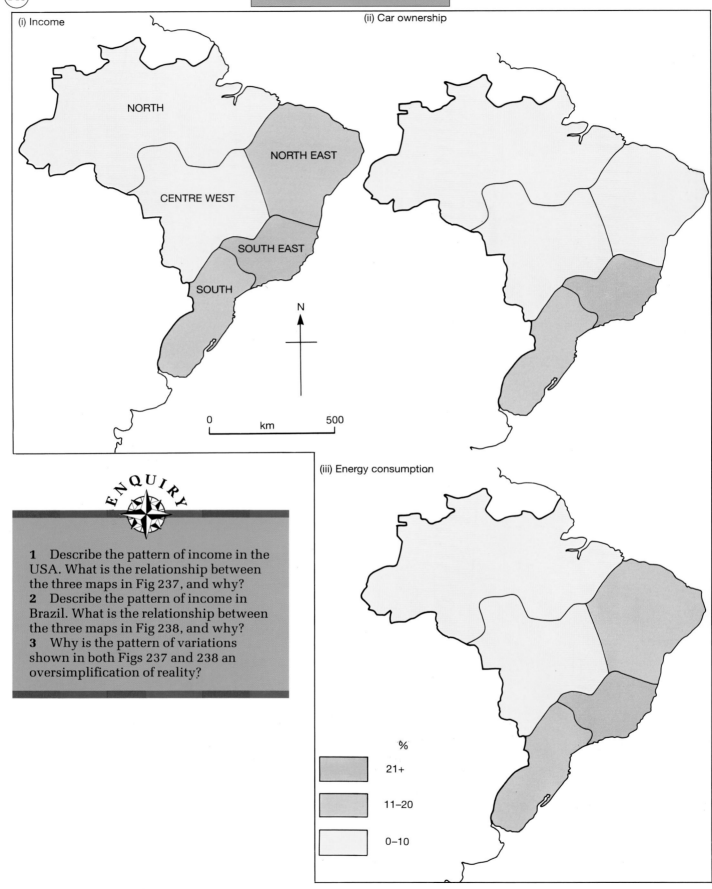

(i) Income

NORTH

NORTH EAST

CENTRE WEST

SOUTH EAST

SOUTH

N

0   km   500

(ii) Car ownership

(iii) Energy consumption

%

21+

11–20

0–10

ENQUIRY

1 Describe the pattern of income in the USA. What is the relationship between the three maps in Fig 237, and why?
2 Describe the pattern of income in Brazil. What is the relationship between the three maps in Fig 238, and why?
3 Why is the pattern of variations shown in both Figs 237 and 238 an oversimplification of reality?

Fig 238   Percentage of Brazil's (i) income; (ii) car ownership and (iii) energy consumption accounted for by region

5.2 How can different levels of development be explained?

A number of theories and models have been put forward to explain the patterns of development described in Section 5.1 and three of these are considered in this Section: dependency theory; the take off model; and the core-periphery model.

Dependency theory

In this theory rich, industrialised countries are called **metropoles** while poor, less industrialised countries are called **satellites**. The metropoles control the satellites and this relationship is called **dependency** (Fig 239).

The dependency theory states that the metropoles of Europe gained a great deal of wealth from their conquest of the New World in the sixteenth and seventeenth centuries and that this helped them to start the process of industrialisation. Setting up industries made them richer and more powerful and stimulated a demand for raw materials and food. They looked to the satellites to provide these products and took them over as **colonies**; for example, in the nineteenth century the UK, France and Germany established large overseas empires. This began the relationship of dependency.

In the 1960s and 1970s most colonies won political independence but they have found that they still depend on the metropoles in many ways; for example, the metropoles provide a market for their raw materials, and loans for development projects. This relationship is unfair because they are caught in the *trade imbalance trap* (which means that they get less for their exports of raw materials than they have to pay for their imports of manufactured goods), and are left with debts which they cannot repay (see Section 5.4).

So, dependency theory explains the North-South development gap by seeing MEDCs as metropoles and LEDCs as satellites. The unequal relationship between North and South – dependency – is because MEDCs have controlled, and still do control, the economies of LEDCs.

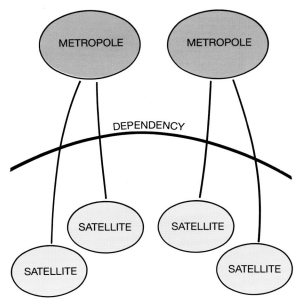

Fig 239   Metropoles, satellites and dependency

ENQUIRY

1 Draw and label a diagram to show how the dependency theory explains the North-South development gap.

2 Which of the following statements support the dependency theory and which disagree with it? In each case, explain your decision.

● Many LEDCs were poor before they became colonies.

● Australia and New Zealand were colonies but they have become prosperous, independent countries.

● Many LEDCs had flourishing civilisations before they became colonies; for example, the Aztecs in Mexico, the Incas in Peru, and the Moghuls in India.

● Some LEDCs were never colonies, or were taken over only for a short period of time, but are very poor; for example, Thailand and Ethiopia.

● The North East of Brazil had the strongest links with Portugal, the former colonial power, and is one of the poorest parts of the country today.

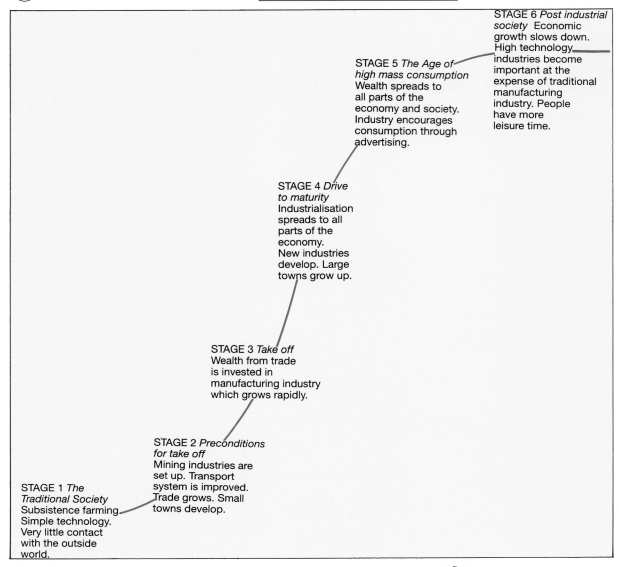

STAGE 6 *Post industrial society* Economic growth slows down. High technology industries become important at the expense of traditional manufacturing industry. People have more leisure time.

STAGE 5 *The Age of high mass consumption* Wealth spreads to all parts of the economy and society. Industry encourages consumption through advertising.

STAGE 4 *Drive to maturity* Industrialisation spreads to all parts of the economy. New industries develop. Large towns grow up.

STAGE 3 *Take off* Wealth from trade is invested in manufacturing industry which grows rapidly.

STAGE 2 *Preconditions for take off* Mining industries are set up. Transport system is improved. Trade grows. Small towns develop.

STAGE 1 *The Traditional Society* Subsistence farming. Simple technology. Very little contact with the outside world.

Fig 240   The take off model of development

The take off model

This states that all countries pass through a series of stages as they develop (Fig 240).

Its explanation for the North-South development gap is simply that the richer countries of the North began the process of development before the poorer countries of the South. However, it suggests that LEDCs will eventually catch up.

Its ideas can also be applied to individual countries. It suggests how and why they have developed; how they are likely to develop in the future; and the sorts of things which could be done to speed up the development process.

ENQUIRY

1 Draw a diagram of the take off model and label it using no more than 12 words for each stage.
2 Read Fig 241. In what ways does the USA's development fit in with the take off model? Are there any ways in which it does not fit in?
3 Read Fig 242. In what ways does Brazil's development fit in with the take off model? Are there any ways in which it does not fit in?
4 What problems do LEDCs face as they begin the process of economic development which MEDCs did not have to face when they industrialised in the nineteenth century?

Economic development in the USA

Before 1565
The first permanent settlement in the USA was St Augustine, in Florida, founded by the Spanish in 1565. Before then, the American Indians led a traditional way of life as subsistence farmers and/or as hunters and gatherers.

1565-1783
During this period, European countries, particularly Britain, established settlements in the east of the continent. The largest of these were ports, such as Boston and New York. They were the main centres of economic development, exporting raw materials such as timber, tobacco and cotton, and importing manufactured goods.

1783-1835
In 1783, the USA won independence from Britain. Economic development was stimulated by the States forging closer links with each other (before, nearly all of their trade had been with Britain); and because a greater percentage of the profits from trade stayed in the country instead of going back to Britain. The developments which took place were mainly to do with exploiting the country's agricultural potential.

1835-1875
This was a very important period because it saw the beginnings of industrialisation. Agriculture stimulated manufacturing industry because it wanted farm machinery in order to increase its productivity. There was also a demand for the products of the industrial revolution from the transport industry because it saw railways as the best way to connect a country which, by 1846, was 35 times the size of Britain. By 1875 the main part of the railway network was complete, including the east coast – west coast link.

1875-1945
In these years, the USA rose to be one of the world's leading industrial nations. Heavy industry became concentrated in the Manufacturing Belt in the north east of the country (see Section 3.8). Henry Ford pioneered the factory assembly line and sold 15 million Model Ts between 1908 and 1928. Large companies began to dominate production; for example, in 1940, 50 per cent of the country's production was accounted for by only one per cent of its companies.

1945-early 1970s
Four major trends can be identified in this period:
● Significant economic growth: it stayed at more than four per cent per annum throughout the whole of the 1960s.
● An increase in wealth; for example, average incomes rose from US$ 2200 in 1947 to US$ 3800 in 1972 in real terms.
● 'Producer services' such as marketing, advertising and research and development increased dramatically; for example, in 1947 they employed six million people but this had risen to 12 million by 1977.
● Traditional manufacturing industries declined; for example, employment in this sector went down from 32 million in 1947 to 24 million in 1977.

1970s onwards
In recent years economic growth has slowed down; imports have been greater than exports; and traditional manufacturing industry has continued to decline. However, there has been growth in light industry and high-technology industry in the 'Sunbelt' of the south and west (see Section 3.8).

Fig 241   Economic development in the USA

Economic development in Brazil

Before 1500
The people who lived in Brazil before the country was discovered by Europeans were subsistence farmers, hunters and gatherers. They lived in tribes very much like the Yanomami Indians of the Amazon rainforest do today.

1500-1822
For nearly 300 years Brazil was a Portuguese colony. The country was exploited, first for sugar and then for gold.

1822-1920s
Although politically independent, Brazil still found itself economically dependent on exporting raw materials, mainly to Europe and North America. In the 1840s coffee plantations were set up and in the early 1900s rubber plantations were established.

1930s-1940s
This period saw the Brazilian Government getting heavily involved in economic development for the first time. It took control of coffee exports so that it could influence the world market and it invested in manufacturing industry; for example, the National Steel Company completed the country's first large integrated iron and steel works at Volta Redonda in 1947.

1950s onwards
Brazil's first development plan was published in 1957 (a). The Government has continued to be involved with industry through state run companies; it has encouraged multinationald to set up; and it has borrowed heavily from MDCs in order to finance development projects. Economic growth rates have been impressive; for example, between 1970 and 1982 the average rate was 7.6 per cent per year compared with 1.9 per cent in the UK. Also, some development has spread to peripheral regions, such as the Amazon rainforest.

However, the majority of the population remain very poor and there are big contrasts within the country (see Fig 238, page 148). Even in the most prosperous part of the country, the South East, there are enormous differences between the wealthy areas of cities such as Rio de Janeiro (b) and its growing shanty towns (c). It has the largest international debt of any country in the world and its economy has suffered from rapid inflation.

(a) Brazil's development plans

Plan	Year	Main aims and objectives
1	1957–61	to develop own industries in order to cut imports;
2	1963–6	to control inflation; to reduce inequalities in regional income; to improve education; to encourage manufacturing industry;
3	1964–66	as for plans 1 and 2 with an emphasis on increasing employment
4	1968–70	as above, with an emphasis on economic growth;
5	1970–72	to correct regional inequalities and the balance between primary, secondary and tertiary industry; to redistribute personal income; to introduce land reform;
6	1972–74	similar to above but no mention of agriculture;
7	1975–79	as above, plus – to improve social and political conditions; to bring agriculture into the development strategy;
8	1980–85	as above, plus – to obtain equal access to social facilities; to encourage and improve agriculture; to reduce the pressures of rural-urban migration.

(b) Downtown Rio de Janeiro (c) A Rio slum (inset)

Fig 242 Economic development in Brazil

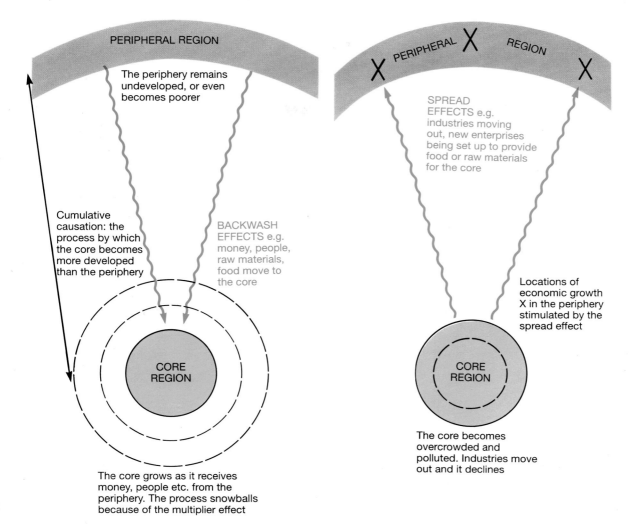

Fig 243 Cumulative causation and backwash effects

Fig 244 Spread effects

The core-periphery model

This model looks at the relationship between prosperous **core regions** and the less prosperous **peripheral regions** which surround them.

It sees the process of development beginning when one region (which becomes the core) finds that it has an advantage over another (which becomes the periphery); for example, a deposit of valuable raw materials, or a new invention. As a result it attracts money and people from the surrounding area and the development process 'snowballs'; more people means a bigger market, which means more demand for goods, which means more factories, which means more demand for labour, which means more people, and so on (this is known as the **multiplier effect**). The whole process by which the core becomes prosperous at the expense of the periphery is called **cumulative causation** (Fig 243).

However, as the core becomes increasingly developed, two things happen which can benefit the periphery: Firstly, the core needs to be supplied with more and more food and raw materials. Secondly, the core becomes overcrowded and polluted and as a result industry begins to move away. Both of these changes can create jobs and wealth in the periphery (Fig 244).

This model explains the North-South development gap by seeing MEDCs as the core and LEDCs as the periphery. The movement of raw materials from South to North is an example of a **backwash effect** while the movement of multinational companies to LEDCs is an example of a **spread effect.**

It explains contrasts in development within countries by seeing prosperous regions as the core and less prosperous regions as the periphery.

ENQUIRY

1 With the help of diagrams, describe and explain the main features of the core-periphery model.

2 Can you think of any other examples of backwash and spread effects which operate at either a global or a national scale?

3 Look back at Figs 237 and 238 and reconsider Figs 241 and 242. Could the core-periphery model help to explain economic development in the USA and Brazil? Give a detailed answer for each country.

4 Go through your answers to all of the questions in this Section and then complete a copy of Fig 245.

	Does it seem best at the national or global scale, or both?	One argument in its favour.	One argument against it.	Overall, do I find it convincing?: yes, no, not sure.
Dependency theory				
Take off model				
Core-periphery model				

Fig 245 Theories and models of development: a summary table

5.3 How are LEDCs meeting the challenge of development?

Agricultural development: the Green Revolution in India

The **Green Revolution** is the phrase used to describe a high technology approach to increasing food production. It has four main characteristics:

- the use of scientifically bred, high yielding varieties of plants (**HYVs**);
- irrigation;
- the use of large quantities of chemical fertiliser;
- the use of chemically produced herbicides, fungicides and pesticides,

Research began in the 1940s in the USA, funded by the Rockefeller foundation. A team of scientists led by Norman Borlaug developed a high yielding variety of wheat which was grown first in Mexico. In the 1960s a plant breeding centre near Manila in the Philippines played a major role in developing new strains of rice. One of the early varieties, IR-8, became known as 'miracle rice' because its yield was five times that of ordinary rice (Fig 246).

In the mid-1960s India was facing serious food shortages because harvests had been badly affected by drought, and because of its rapidly expanding population. Shipments of grain, mainly from the USA, prevented famine and the Indian Government set up a programme to introduce the new types of wheat and rice so that the country would be able to feed itself in the future. By 1979 nearly three quarters of the area used for growing wheat and nearly half the area used for growing rice was under HYVs.

India's Green Revolution has undoubtedly produced some impressive results. Food production has increased significantly (Fig 247) and, except when the monsoon rains fail, the country enjoys a food surplus.

However, there have been problems. HYVs need large inputs of chemical fertiliser, as well as herbicides, fungicides and pesticides. The cost of these inputs has cancelled out the increased income from the higher yields.

Fig 246 Miracle rice

Small-scale farmers have had problems paying for these inputs: many have had to take out loans and when they have been unable to pay them back they have had to sell some of their land, usually to wealthier, large-scale farmers. The result has been an increase in the number of landless peasants, a decrease in the overall number of farms and an increase in the average size of farm.

HYVs also need plenty of water and this has caused environmental problems. In some places irrigation has produced serious waterlogging. In others salt has been drawn to

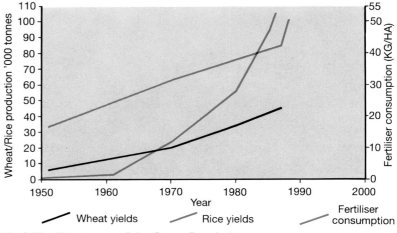

Fig 247 The impact of the Green Revolution

the surface as the irrigation water has evaporated and made the soil completely infertile, a process known as 'salination'. Village wells have run dry as the water table has been tapped. Rivers, lakes and the water table itself have been polluted by concentrations of fertiliser in the run-off from the fields.

Some experts have argued that it would have been better if money had been invested in improved storage facilities because at the moment nearly 25 per cent of all food produced is eaten by rats before it is ready to be used.

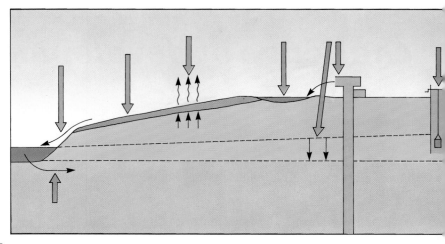

Fig 248   Irrigation problems

ENQUIRY

1   Explain what you understand by the phrase 'the Green Revolution'.
2   Describe the trends shown in Fig 237 and comment on the relationship between fertiliser consumption and wheat/rice yields.
3   What has been the main advantage of the Green Revolution?
4   Why has the Green Revolution resulted in 'an increase in the number of landless peasants, a decrease in the overall number of farms and an increase in the average size of farm'?
5   Copy Fig 248 and add onto it in the correct places the following labels:
    – fertiliser in run-off from fields pollutes river;
    – irrigation water evaporates and draws salt to the surface;
    – the water table becomes polluted;
    – village well dries up;
    – diesel-powered 'tube well' lowers the water table;
    – salt crust makes land infertile;
    – waterlogging takes land out of production.
6   With hindsight, was the Green Revolution a good idea? Justify your opinion.

Industrial development: the Newly Industrialising Countries of East Asia

A number of LEDCs have made manufacturing industry the most important part of their development programme. They have become known as 'Newly Industrialising Countries' (**NICs**) and have two main characteristics:

- manufacturing output and exports have grown much faster in recent years than in MEDCs;
- their development strategy has been geared towards the export of manufactured goods.

The first countries of East Asia to industrialise (after Japan) were Singapore, South Korea, Hong Kong and Taiwan. Their economic development has been spectacular; for example, between 1960 and 1980 their manufactured exports grew at an average rate of 28 per cent per year. Other indicators are given in Fig 249.

A number of factors help to explain their success. All have been able to take advantage of a plentiful supply of cheap labour. The governments of South Korea, Taiwan and Singapore, in particular, have played a major role in organising and helping manufacturing industry. Singapore and Hong Kong were already major ports and this helped them to develop trade links. South Korea and Taiwan benefited from western aid because of their resistance to their communist neighbours, North Korea and China. All have benefited from foreign investment and their own governments have invested in education and training.

In the 1960s the NICs developed labour-intensive industries such as textiles and clothing. This led to job losses in MEDCs because it was cheaper to import these goods than to make them. However, it was a period of economic growth and most of those who became unemployed found new jobs quite quickly.

However, in the 1980s the four NICs found themselves in a new situation. Firstly, many MEDCs put up trade barriers, such as quotas and tariffs, to protect their own industries because the world recession was causing rising unemployment. Secondly, they faced competition from countries like Malaysia and Indonesia who were beginning industrialisation programmes of their own and were able to produce even cheaper goods, mainly because of lower wage rates.

Fig 249 NICs of East Asia: development indicators

	Population (millions)	Population growth rate	GNP per capita (US $)	% of national income accounted for by		GDP average annual growth per year %				Trade surplus/ deficit millions (US $) 1992
				manufacturing industry	agriculture	1960-67	1967-73	1970-82	1980-91	
Singapore	2.8	1.5	12 890	38	<1	7.5	13.0	8.5	4.9	−8710
South Korea	44.2	1.1	6340	45	8	7.2	10.9	8.6	8.8	−9659 (1991)
Hong Kong	5.9	1.2	13 200	25	<1	9.9	10.2	9.9	5.4	−3917
Taiwan	21.0	1.3	8000	43	4	8.9 (GNP)	10.6 (GNP)	8.7 (GNP)	8.0	9493

Fig 250 The redevelopment of Singapore's CBD

began to develop itself as a financial centre and this led to the demolition of slums to make way for a new central business district (Fig 250).

They responded by developing **capital-intensive industries** such as machinery and high-technology electronic equipment; for example, in 1980 Taiwan's Government set up a science park which by 1991 had 111 factories and 16 000 employees. Singapore

Overall, it has been estimated that the number of jobs lost in MEDCs because of trade with the NICs has been cancelled out by the number of jobs gained. On the one hand, cheap imports have contributed towards the decline of a number of traditional industries such as textiles, ship-building and vehicle manufacture while on the other, the NICs have imported a large amount of machinery, equipment and components from MEDCs (Fig 251).

In conclusion, the economies of East Asia's first four NICs remain strong although forecasts of economic growth are lower than in the past; there have been major problems, such as the stock market crash in Taiwan in 1990 which wiped 70 per cent off the value of its shares; and there is uncertainty about the future of Hong Kong when it is returned to China in 1997.

ENQUIRY

1   With reference to Fig 249, explain why Singapore, South Korea, Hong Kong and Taiwan are classified as NICs.
2   Why have these four NICs been so successful?
3   Explain why their economies have developed.
4   Draw a flow line map to show the main markets for Taiwan's exports in 1989 (Fig 252). Use a scale of 1mm = 3 per cent. Describe and explain the pattern your map shows.
5   What evidence is there in Fig 251 to support the view that the overall effect on number of jobs lost in MEDCs because of trade with NICs has been cancelled out by the number of jobs gained?
6   Why might it be more difficult for an LEDC to achieve the success of East Asia's first four NICs if it starts on an industrialisation programme now?

Appropriate technology

Some people think that big schemes like the Aswan Dam project in Egypt are the wrong sort of developments for LEDCs because, for example, they are so expensive, they require the involvement of foreign companies and they rarely give direct help to the poor.
Appropriate technology is the phrase used to describe developments which are considered to be more suitable for these countries. The characteristics of appropriate technology are compared with those of advanced technology industry in Fig 253.

	Exports	Imports
Hong Kong	USA China UK	China Japan USA
Taiwan	USA Japan Hong Kong	Japan USA Kuwait
South Korea	USA Japan Hong Kong	Japan USA Malaysia
Singapore	USA Malaysia Japan	Japan USA Malaysia

(Countries are listed in order of importance)

Fig 251   Main trading partners of the NICs

Country	%
USA	39
Japan	15
Hong Kong	9
Germany	4
UK	3
Singapore	3
Canada	3
Australia	2

Fig 252   Main markets for Taiwan's exports 1989

Appropriate technology	Advanced technology
smaller-scale	larger-scale
cheaper equipment	expensive equipment
small demand for energy	big demand for energy
large demand for labour	employs fewer workers
uses local resources	often needs imported raw materials
involves traditional skills	needs training in new skills

Fig 253   Comparing appropriate and advanced technology

Fig 255 Combine harvester

Fig 254 Commune thresher

Fig 254 is a photograph of a rice threshing machine being used on a farm in China. The traditional way of threshing rice (which means separating the grain from the stem of the plant) is by beating it against the ground. The threshing machine is operated by hand and is quicker and more efficient than this traditional method. However, compare this simple piece of locally-made technology with the combine harvester in Fig 255 which cuts, threshes and bails; and costs £50 000 if you buy one new.

Fig 256 is a photograph of a shoe factory in rural China. The operation is well-organised and the workers are skilled at their job. However, it uses local raw materials and it requires little machinery. This is very different to, say, a microchip factory in Hong Kong.

Fig 256 Commune shoe factory, Chonquing

ENQUIRY

1 Explain what you understand by the term 'appropriate technology'.

2 Consider the following industrial factors:
  – large amounts of labour;
  – plenty of people with money to buy things;
  – traditional skills;
  – plenty of capital;
  – few people with money to buy things;
  – well-developed services, such as electricity supply.

a) Which of these factors are characteristics of MEDCs?

b) Which of these factors are characteristics of LEDCs?

c) Which of these factors are necessary for advanced technology industry?

d) Which of these factors suit appropriate technology?

e) Which type of technology do the answers to these questions suggest would be best for **i)** MEDCs and **ii)** LEDCs?

3 Compare either the threshing machine and a combine harvester or the shoe factory and a microchip factory under the following headings:
  – inputs (e.g. local or imported raw materials?);
  – processes (e.g. simple or technical?);
  – outputs (e.g. high or low productivity per person?).

4 Appropriate technology has its disadvantages as well as its advantages. Make a list of at least ten advanced technology products an LEDC is likely to need and will therefore have to import if it cannot produce them itself. Two possibilities to get you started are iron and steel and motor vehicles.

5 Are the products of appropriate technology likely to lead to the development of an export market? Explain your answer.

5.4 Foreign aid – who really benefits?

Who gives aid, and what is it spent on?

Foreign aid is help given by one country or group of people to another country or group of people. In 1991 the world's 18 richest countries gave or lent about £30 000 million to the 50 poorest countries. However, the number of people in need of help continues to rise.

There are two main sources of aid. Firstly, governments give aid as part of their overall spending programme. This aid is either given to governments directly (**bilateral aid**) or it is given to international aid organisations like the World Bank (**multilateral aid**). Secondly, charities and voluntary organisations like Oxfam or Save the Children collect money and organise their own aid programmes (**voluntary aid**).

Most aid is given by MEDCs to LEDCs. However, LEDCs have helped each other on a number of occasions; for example, China helped Tanzania and Zambia to build the Tan Zam railway which allows Zambia to export its copper through the port of Dar es Salaam.

The UK's aid budget is shown in Fig 257. Government aid is 0.3 per cent of GNP which is well below the target of 1 per cent set by the Brandt Commission in 1980.

Not all of the money raised as aid goes directly to the people who need it. Governments and charities (Fig 158) have costs which they must meet if they are to work efficiently.

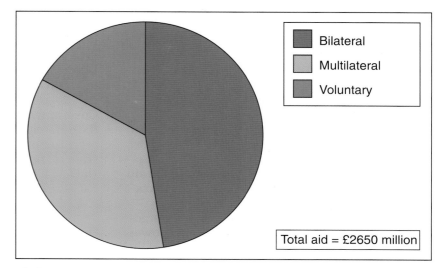

Fig 257 The UK's overseas aid budget, 1992

Legend:
- Bilateral
- Multilateral
- Voluntary

Total aid = £2650 million

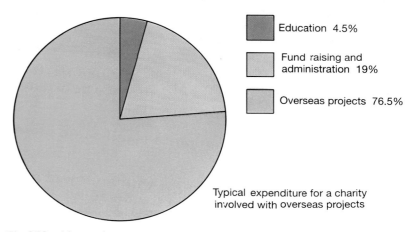

Fig 258 How aid is spent

Legend:
- Education 4.5%
- Fund raising and administration 19%
- Overseas projects 76.5%

Typical expenditure for a charity involved with overseas projects

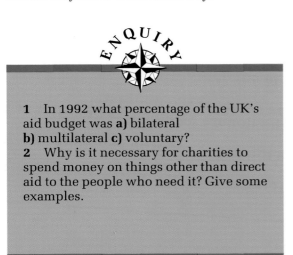

ENQUIRY

1   In 1992 what percentage of the UK's aid budget was **a)** bilateral **b)** multilateral **c)** voluntary?
2   Why is it necessary for charities to spend money on things other than direct aid to the people who need it? Give some examples.

Types of aid

There are many different types of aid and the relationships between them are shown in Fig 259.

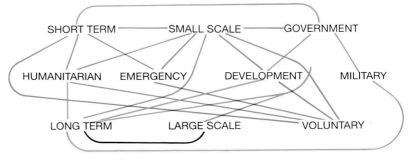

Fig 259 Types of aid

Short-term aid copes with the immediate needs of a crisis; for example, providing food for people in a famine, or shelter for people who have been made homeless in an earthquake. Long-term aid helps people in the years to come; for example, by irrigating land so that it can be farmed, or by building new homes designed to stand up to all but the worst earthquake.

Small-scale aid usually involves a small amount of money and affects a limited number of people. However, it can be of great benefit to those who receive it. The women's group in Thailand described in Section 3.2 is an example of this type of aid. Large-scale aid involves large amounts of money and affects many people, although it does not always help the poorest: the UK Government's largest donation in 1989 was £63 million for a power station in Bangladesh – but the majority of the country's population do not have electricity in their homes.

Aid can also be classified according to what it is spent on. Food, health care, industry and agriculture are all targets for aid. Military aid is always controversial. For example the United Nations gave humanitarian aid (food, medical supplies etc) to the Bosnian Muslims during the siege of Sarajevo in 1993 but it decided not to give them arms even though this would have helped them to defend themselves.

Governments involve themselves with all of the different types of aid. Voluntary organisations usually concentrate on small-scale aid because of their limited funds. However, Fig 260 suggests that this is not necessarily a disadvantage.

Fig 260   Oxfam's aims

AID

Aid can be vitally important to the poorest people. It can be a lifeline to those whose resources are draining away. But there is a difference between voluntary aid given by organisations like Oxfam, and aid given by governments:

The aid that OXFAM gives supports small scale projects which help local communties.

- **TARGETED AID:**
  In Bangladesh, Oxfam helps with a project designed to provide treatment and training appropriate to the needs of the disabled.
- **COUNTERING INAPPROPRIATE AID:**
  In Brazil, Oxfam works with groups whose futures are threatened by large scale development.
- **AID WITHOUT STRINGS:**
  In Kampuchea, Oxfam is involved in providing water supplies for villagers.

This is aid which is appropriate to the needs of the poor.

- **GOVERNMENT aid too can really help.** But often it is not appropriate to the needs of the poorest.
- it often funds large scale projects which ignore the needs of the poorest.
- it often is involved in the commercial needs of the donors as much as benefits of the recipients.
- it often is political — given to governments which the donor countries support.

OXFAM aims to give appropriate aid to the most needy; regardless of political or commercial considerations.

Aid and debt

A major aid issue at the present time is **international debt**. In the mid-1970s large amounts of money were deposited in Western banks by the oil producing countries. A great deal of this was lent by the banks to LEDCs: the banks wanted to earn interest by lending the money and the LEDCs wanted the money for their development programmes.

However, in the 1980s the LEDCs earnt less and less from their exports, mainly because of the world recession (see Section 6.3) and they found it increasingly difficult to pay back the money they had borrowed.

Over 50 countries had to go to the International Monetary Fund (IMF) for help. They were given further loans but only if they agreed to 'spend less, and earn more'. In practice this usually meant using more land to grow export crops rather than subsistence crops; cutting food subsidies and spending less on health care; consequently, the poor saw their standard of living fall still further.

By 1987 LEDCs owed more than £1100 billion and most of them were unable to pay back even the annual interest charges. In fact, the money they were repaying was greater than the amount they were receiving in aid (Fig 261). The Western banks were also becoming concerned that they might not get their money back. For example, Peru failed to pay back a loan to the IMF in 1986 and although it was banned from receiving further loans there was very little else that could be done about it.

Further measures have been taken. The World Bank has given low interest loans to certain countries; debts have been re-scheduled,

which means that they can be paid back at a later date; and some debts have been written off completely. However, the problem has not been solved and the world's poorest countries are still having to spend a large percentage of their earnings on repaying loans taken out nearly 20 years ago.

	1982	1983	1984	1985	1986
Aid to LEDCs	117.8	97.7	86.1	82.3	84.7
Debt repayment by LEDCs	131.6	131.5	131.7	140.7	152.8
Net flow of money from LEDCs to MEDCs	13.8	33.8	45.6	58.4	68.1

(Figures in US $ billions.)

Fig 261 Aid and debt in the early 1980s

Should we give foreign aid at all?

This is not a new question. In England in the nineteenth century there were fierce arguments as to whether or not the church should send missionaries abroad or concentrate its efforts on improving the terrible conditions a great number of poor people were living in at home.

Having worked through this section, you should be in a good position to make up your own mind. Clearly, the people in Fig 262 have very different opinions!

We should help people in need whoever they are.

Everyone needs a helping hand at times.

The earth is our home and we should help all people who live on it.

What happens in the LEDCs is bound to affect us because the North and South are so closely linked.

If we help LEDCs it will improve our international relations.

If we help LEDCs it will provide new markets for our manufactured goods.

We've helped to make their problems because when these countries were colonies we turned them into producers of cheap primary exports.

Anyway, the **poor** people of these countries cannot be blamed for their problems.

The least we can do is to help them to stand on their own two feet again.

People should help themselves.

If we help them once they will expect us to do it again.

We should help the poor people at home first.

Nonsense – we are quite capable of surviving without LEDCs.

These countries are not important – it's the powerful countries who count.

These countries are too poor to buy much – it would be better to sell more to Europe.

They were better off when they were colonies – nobody starved then.

Yes they can – they're lazy and they haven't controlled their population growth.

It won't work – they're not clever enough to look after themselves, so why waste time trying?

Fig 262   Should we give aid?

1   Which of the two arguments used by the woman for giving aid are the most convincing?
2   Which of the two arguments used by the man against giving aid are the most convincing?
3   Suggest three situations when you would give aid. Compare your list and reasons with the rest of the group.

5.5 Assessment task: *Breaking poverty's grip*

Bangladesh is a densely populated country, much of which occupies the delta of the rivers Ganges and Brahmaputra (Fig 263). It has a monsoon climate and it is often battered by cyclones which move north along the Bay of Bengal in late spring and early autumn (Fig 264).

It is a poor country which is heavily dependent upon agriculture (Fig 265). The soils of the delta are very fertile but agricultural development has been hampered by many factors such as drought, floods, uneconomic holdings and traditional, labour-intensive methods.

When this part of Asia gained independence from the UK in 1947, Bangladesh – then known as East Bengal – became a province of Pakistan. The reason for making it part of a country over 2000 km away was that its population was mainly Moslem, as was Pakistan's whereas India was mainly Hindu. However, it felt ignored by Pakistan and, after a bitter civil war which left one million people dead, it achieved independence in December 1971.

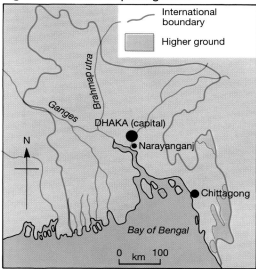

Fig 263   Location map: Bangladesh

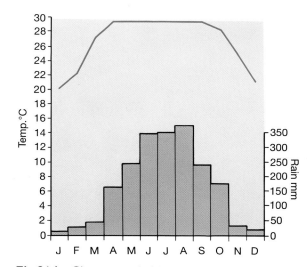

Fig 264   Climate graph: Narayanganj

The war of independence had left the country in ruins and it was in desperate need of foreign aid. Emergency relief helped to cope with the immediate crisis. Long-term relief followed with the aim of putting the country

Area	144 000 km^2
Population	122.3 million
Population increase	2.5 per cent per year
GNP	220 US $ per person per year
Source of GNP a) agriculture b) manufacturing c) services	 36% 16% 48%
Food supply	2037 calories per person per day
Main exports	jute and jute products
Main destination of exports	USA, Italy, Japan
Main imports	machinery, food
Main source of imports	Japan, USA, UAE
Trade deficit	1716 million US $ (1991)

Fig 265   Bangladesh: fact file

back on its own two feet. Since then, over $25 billion of aid has been given but Bangladesh remains one of the poorest countries in the world (Fig 266). This begs the question, why has aid largely failed?

Some of the money has been wasted on badly planned projects. For example, the Meghna Dhanagoda Project aimed to stop flooding where the Ganges and Brahmaputra meet by building an embankment (Fig 267). However, the foreign development agencies – because of lack of consultation with the local experts – did not realise how often the rivers on the delta change their course. Consequently, the embankment was built in the wrong place and, rather than stopping floods from reaching fields, it has trapped water on them.

Some of the money has been spent on inappropriate projects. For example, a development bank loaned several million pounds for the building of a factory to manufacture high technology lenses used in eye surgery. However, there is no home market for such an expensive product and it has yet to start production. On the other hand, relatively inexpensive shelters would have saved the lives of many of the 140 000 people who died in a cyclone in April 1991 (Fig 268).

Some aid seems to have helped the donor as much as Bangladesh. For example, the UK has given badly needed help to tea estates in the north of the country. However, much of the aid has been in the form of loans so it will, eventually, have to be paid back; 40 per cent of the money given for buying equipment has been spent with British firms; and part of the aid budget pays for the wages of the consultants, most of whom are British.

Country	GNP per person per year (US $), 1991
Madagascar	210
Burundi	210
Sierra Leone	210
Cambodia	200
Guinea-Bissau	190
Nepal	180
Somalia	150
Ethiopia	120
Tanzania	100
Mozambique	70

Fig 266   The world's poorest countries

Fig 267   Ganges River

Fig 268   April 1991 cyclone: Sandwip, South Bangladesh

A great deal of the money has found its way into the pockets of the rich, rather than the poor. Sometimes this has been because of the type of aid. For example, the introduction of High Yielding Varieties of seed has increased crop production but this has benefited land owners and not the majority of the population who are landless peasants. Too often, it has been because of theft and corruption. Also, arranging loans has become big business: the brokers who bring donors and development projects together receive commission which comes directly, or indirectly, from the aid budget and it has been estimated that 60-70 per cent of all upper incomes in Bangladesh are earnt in this way.

Many people – in Bangladesh and abroad – think that a large part of the problem has been too much aid, rather than too little, because it has reduced the need for the country to do things for itself. For example, it has one of the lowest rates of tax collection of any LEDC and its civil service is one of the largest: by increasing the former and reducing the latter it could raise, and save, money for itself.

The success of the Grameen Bank suggests another possible way forward. It is a new bank which has grown rapidly and now has branches in one third of the country's villages. It makes small loans but these allow the villagers to buy what they need to be more independent; for example, £75 buys a cow and the sale of milk means that a family can support itself, and pay back the loan. These loans also allow the purchase of appropriate technology which, in turn, can encourage the development of co-operatives like the women's group in Thailand (page 95) and the Mujurpet project in India (page 183).

The big aid donors are tending to set more conditions before they give aid, in an attempt to make sure that it is spent on what it is meant for. They are also making greater use of local organisations with direct links to the poor. For its part, the Government of Bangladesh would like to have more control over how the money is spent but it is still so dependent on aid that it cannot afford to upset potential donors by dictating terms.

Task

Imagine that you are secretary of the schools' Charity Committee. At a recent meeting, the Committee decided that it would like to be part of the Oxfam Project Partners scheme and to sponsor the development project in Bangladesh (Fig 269).

Your task is to write to the Headteacher explaining why the Committee thinks that this is a good project for the school to support. Your letter should include the following:

1   A brief account of what Bangladesh is like – its relief, climate and main land uses.
2   Some carefully chosen statistics to show the development gap between Bangladesh and the UK.
3   An explanation of some of the reasons why Bangladesh is such a poor country.
4   Details of the amount and type of aid the country has received in the last 20 years, and a comment on who or what has benefited most from the different types of aid.
5   An evaluation of the overall effect of aid to Bangladesh: has it been good or bad?
6   A justification of why you think the Oxfam Project Partners scheme is a good way to help the country.

Oxfam Project Partners

OXFAM PROJECT PARTNERS is a unique way in which you can help poor people.

It gives you the chance to see what your regular support for a particular community can achieve.

You'll receive regular updates and reports on your chosen project, and on other vital projects selected for support. You'll be sent interviews, information and pictures so you can follow the project's progress – and share in both the problems and the successes.

And you'll always know exactly how your money is being used. Because Oxfam undertakes to give you yearly accounts detailing the work you are supporting.

No more than 10% will go towards fundraising and administration costs.

Help break poverty's grip in rural Bangladesh

In Bangladesh, nearly everyone relies on agriculture for a living. Thousands of people in the northern area of Dinajpur are dependent on often unscrupulous land owners and "wages" that may only consist of two meals for a long day's work.

As an Oxfam Project Partner you'll be helping local people start co-operative groups, where they can learn how to read, make crafts and look after livestock. You'll help individuals find alternative ways to earn a living, and break out of poverty's grip.

Fig 269   Oxfam Project Partners

MOVEMENT

6.1 What is the best way of getting around?

Transport developments in the UK

Until the nineteenth century all methods of transport were slow. Most roads were in a very poor condition and goods could be moved no faster than by horse and cart. Large, heavy loads could only be transported by boat or barge at sea, or along navigable rivers.

However, the industrial revolution created a demand for better methods of transport. The new industries needed to move large quantities of raw materials and finished products, and many were a long way from the sea.

The first development was the canal system. The Manchester-Bridgewater canal was started in 1761 and in less than 50 years 2500 miles of canal had been built. It was now possible to move materials and goods around the country. However, the barges, pulled by horses, were slow. Also, hills and valleys were major obstacles – even a gentle slope required a flight of locks (Fig 270) – so the engineers took long and winding routes to keep the canals on level ground.

Next came the railway system. The Stockton and Darlington railway was opened in 1825 and by 1850 rail was the most important method of transport for materials, goods and people. The railways had several advantages over the canals: they were quicker; they could take a more direct route because they could cope with steeper slopes; and they were cheaper to build. Engineering skills had also improved and some remarkable viaducts (Fig 271) and tunnels were built to carry the lines to their destinations.

Fig 270 The Grand Union Canal: Foxton Staircase Locks, Leicestershire

Fig 271 Ribblehead viaduct, North Yorkshire

MOVEMENT

Road transport became more important with the development of cars, buses and lorries but it was not until the 1960s that road began to challenge rail as the main method of transport for materials and goods, as well as people. However, by the end of the 1980s, 80 per cent of all freight movements and 90 per cent of all personal journeys were by road. A number of reasons help to explain this development:

• A network of motorways has been built: the first to be opened was the M1 between London and Birmingham in 1959 (Fig 272) and by 1970 all major cities were connected. Journeys by motorways are usually quicker and cheaper than going by rail. Also, modern engineering has allowed motorways to follow more direct routes than the railways.
• Heavy industry has declined so there is less demand for the railways to move heavy, bulky raw materials and finished products. However, light industry has expanded and its raw materials and finished products are more suitable for road transport.
• Larger lorries have been developed.
• The government has invested more money in roads than in the railways.

Fig 272   The M1 in Hertfordshire

However, motorways have their disadvantages; for example, they take up more land than a railway and they cause more noise and air pollution. Plans to build new motorways often cause great controversy (Fig 273).

Fig 273   Protesting against the widening of the M25

Crossing the Pennines

Until the nineteenth century the Pennines were crossed only by footpaths and cart tracks. However, the industrial revolution saw the development of major manufacturing centres in the West Riding of Yorkshire and in the mill towns of Lancashire. This created a demand for better transport links so that the two regions could trade with each other and, in particular, so that the factories of the West Riding could use the port of Liverpool.

The first development was the Leeds-Liverpool canal which was opened in 1816 (Fig 274). It took 2½ days to get from Leeds to Manchester but it gave the region the link it needed. Only 20 years later, in 1836, the Leeds-Liverpool railway was opened; this cut the journey time from Leeds to Manchester to 2½ hours and it soon became more important than the canal. The most recent link is the M62 (Fig 275); is now takes only 40 minutes to get from Leeds to Manchester and a steady stream of vehicles crosses the Pennines, except in the severest of winter weather. The following Enquiry will help you to explore these developments in more detail.

ENQUIRY

1 Look at Fig 276. What is the straight line distance, in kilometres, from Leeds to Liverpool? Compare this with the distance by **a)** canal, **b)** railway and **c)** motorway. Why is the canal route so much longer than the other routes? Why is the railway longer than the motorway?
2 Why does the motorway avoid the main towns?
3 Why did the railway replace the canal as the most important way of crossing the Pennines? Why has it, in turn, been replaced by the motorway?
4 Read Fig 277. Why does the Department of Transport want to build a new section of motorway? Explain, in detail, why local people are opposed to both of the routes. What do you think should happen?

Fig 274   Leeds-Liverpool canal, Skipton

Fig 275   M62 Leeds to Manchester

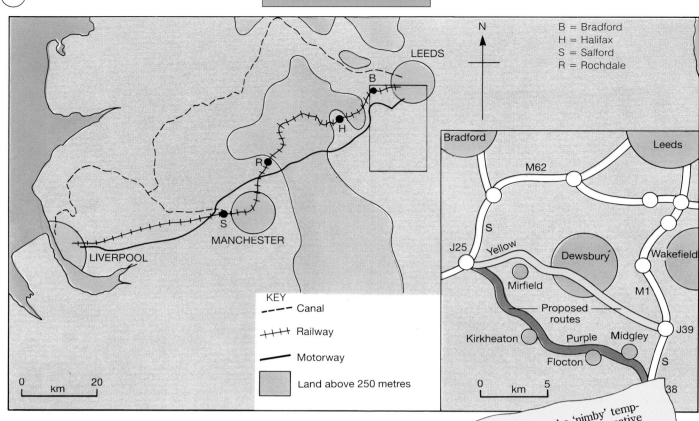

Fig 276   Routeways across the Pennines

'M25 of North' fear as new M1 link plans march onward

A SHORT motorway spur which would save drivers 10 minutes but destroy up to 50 properties and a wedge of green belt is threating to turn into a Northern equivalent of Twyford Down.

Attitudes are hardening to the proposed 10-mile traffic relief link between the M1 and M62 in West Yorkshire, put forward because of congestion at the existing Lofthouse interchange where turning traffic regularly queues back on to both motorways.

Conservative and Labour MPs have joined Wakefield and Kirklees councils in opposing both alternative routes put forward by the Department of Transport. A petition of 20,000 names has gone to Parliament and talks have been held with campaigners from the nearby Aire Valley, where protesters wrecked a road inquiry in the 1970s.

"We have 15 separate action groups from communities affected by the two routes", said Charles Elstone, a retired ICI project engineer, pointing out a landmark on the northerly 'yellow' route which would cut through the heavily-populated Calder Valley.

"This is the place where Onward Christian Soldiers was written and sung as a way of getting the children up the hill to Sunday school at Horbury church. The yellow route slices right through it," he said.

The valley has changed since the Rev Sabine Baring Gould and Sir Arthur Sullivan composed the hymn, largely through multi-million pound landscaping by British Coal which has restored fields and copses on the sites of closed collieries.

The Council for the Protection of Rural England, which fears the Department of Transport's overall plans for the area amount to an "M25 of the North" describes the valley as "the backbone of the local green belt areas', and lists canalside walks, a bird sanctuary, and a network of ancient woodland which would be destroyed.

Protests are equally strong along the southern 'purple' route, which cuts through similar pit restoration land at the old Shuttle Eye colliery and a rich agricultural area. Campaigners have resisted the 'nimby' temptation to back the alternative which does not affect their particular backyard, and posters throughout the area urge "Oppose *both* routes."

The £130 million link is promoted by the department as an aid to the local economy. But only 50 of the 2,000 member-firms of Kirklees chamber of commerce have backed the road, and some lorry drivers have criticised it at public meetings.

Unless the transport department abandons the M1-M62 link, the preferred route will be announced this summer when protests will be ratcheted up again.

The Guardian, 20 April 1993

Fig 277   'M25 of North' fear

6.2 What impact do transport developments have?

Seaport developments in the UK

International trade has been important to the UK's economy for hundreds of years. In medieval times, trade with Europe helped the ports of the south and east coast to flourish. In the eighteenth century trade with the New World saw the rise of ports such as Bristol and Liverpool. In the nineteenth century, trade with the colonies – importing food and raw materials and exporting manufactured goods – helped London to become the biggest port in Europe (Fig 278).

Seaports were an excellent location for many industries. They were a **break of bulk point** where goods were unloaded, so if processing was required it was the ideal place because it saved the cost of transporting the materials any further. They also generated their own manufacturing requirements – e.g. ships, engines and cranes – and this helps to explain why, for example, Clydeside produced 50 per cent of the world's shipping tonnage in 1914.

However, the last 50 years have seen major developments, and their nature and impact is examined below.

Fig 278   The Pool of London from London Bridge August 1925

Until the 1950s most vessels were between 4000 and 10 000 tonnes and most goods were loaded and unloaded by hand, which was a slow process. This system meant high labour costs, high port fees and less time at sea. In the 1950s labour costs began to rise and the shipping industry began to look for ways of saving money.

One major development has been an increase in the size of vessel: this has produced economies of scale, i.e. it is cheaper to transport 100 000 tonnes of cargo in one vessel than in two. Oil tankers are now as large as 500 000 tonnes and bulk carriers are as large as 350 000 tonnes.

This, in turn, has led to an increase in **transhipment** which is when a large cargo is offloaded at a main port and taken to its final destination by smaller ships. Rotterdam has become the centre for transhipment in Europe because it is the only port big enough to handle vessels of more than 350 000 tonnes.

Another development has been the growth of **containerisation**. Containers are large metal boxes of a standard size (Fig 279) and they have many advantages:

- Security is better because goods can be packed at the factory itself and then the container can be locked until it reaches its final destination.
- They can be quickly and easily loaded and unloaded by crane.
- They can be unloaded straight onto the lorry or train which is to take them to their final destination, so the goods do not have to be stored in a warehouse.

Associated with containerisation has been the development of the **roll-on/roll-off** ferry (Fig 280). This allows lorries to drive on and off a vessel without having to be loaded or unloaded. Thus, 'through traffic' takes goods direct from the supplier to the customer, and seaports cease to be break of bulk points.

Fig 281 shows the increase in container and roll-on/roll-off traffic, and the decrease in traditional traffic, between 1965 and 1986. It also shows the increase in fuel traffic which has been another major development of the period and which is accounted for by increased exports of North Sea oil from ports such as Sullom Voe.

These developments have had a number of impacts, some for the worse and some for the

Fig 279 Containers being loaded: Oakland, California

Fig 280 Dover: trucks leaving

better. The increase in the size of vessels has led to the closure of many small docks. Those on tidal rivers, such as the Thames, have been most affected because they were already at the head of navigation, i.e. as far upstream as ocean-going vessels could get (Fig 282).

This, in turn, has caused job losses, both in the docks and in the industries associated with the docks, such as food processing. In London's Docklands job losses have been on such a massive scale that the whole character of the areas has changed (Fig 283).

On the other hand, new facilities have been built to cope with the increase in container and roll-on/roll-off traffic. This has created jobs although the mechanised nature of the work means that far fewer dock workers are needed than before.

Some of these container terminals are downstream of the old docks, like Tilbury on the Thames. Others are in new locations. For example, the East Anglian ports of Felixstowe (Fig 284) and Harwich increased their trade by 123 per cent between 1976 and 1986 and now

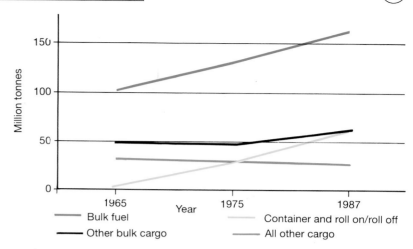

Fig 281 Seaport traffic 1965-1986

Fig 282 Closure of London's docks

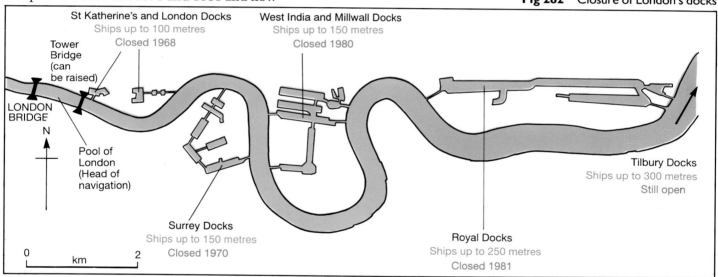

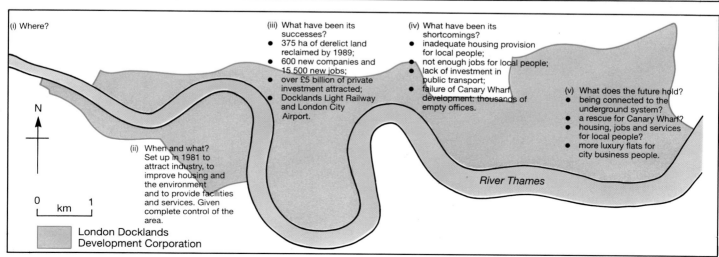

Fig 283 London Docklands Development Corporation: fact file

account for 28 per cent of all the UK's container traffic. They have become particularly important for trade with the EU.

Transhipment has had the effect of increasing trade for a number of small ports such as Selby on the Ouse and Gainsborough on the Trent. They serve a local hinterland and specialise in handling grain, fertiliser, animal feedstuffs, timber and fuel. These ports are economic to run because the vessels are well-designed (e.g. they have large hatches so that cargo can be dealt with quickly); mechanisation helps with the rapid handling of cargo; and labour costs are lower than in the big ports.

The increase in fuel traffic has also brought its advantages and disadvantages. On the one hand, it has generated a great deal of income and boosted the economy of places such as Sullom Voe. On the other, it has increased the risk of pollution. Fortunately, accidents like the *Braer* tanker disaster in January 1993 are infrequent but small spills – accidental and deliberate – have had serious consequences for beaches and wildlife; Milford Haven and the Thames Estuary are two places which have been affected in this way.

Fig 284   Felixstowe container port

ENQUIRY

1   Explain what is meant by the following terms/phrases (the glossary will help you): break of bulk point; head of navigation; draught; hinterland; transhipment; container; roll-on/roll-off ferry.
2   Why have vessels increased in size?
3   What are the main advantages of containerisation?
4   Describe and briefly explain, the changes shown in Fig 281.
5   Why are many ports no longer break of bulk points?
6   Explain the pattern of dock closures in London.
7   Why have small ports been able to expand in recent years?
8   Complete a copy of Fig 285 to summarise the impacts of seaport developments in the UK.
9   Write an account of London's Docklands using the following headings: What was it like? Why did the docks close? What problems were caused by their closure? How has the government tried to help the area? What changes have taken place? Have they been for better or worse? What does the future hold?
Fig 283 will get you started but you will need to carry out your own research as well.

Fig 285   Summary table: seaport developments in the UK

	Increase in size of vessels	Development of containerisation and roll-on/roll-off terminals	Transhipment	Fuel traffic
Advantages	1 Transport has become _____ .	1 _____ have been created. 2 Loading and unloading is _____ .	1 Trade at small ports has _____ .	1 The _____ of some areas e.g. Sullom Voe have benefited.
Disadvantages	1 Many docks have _____ . 2 _____ have been lost. 3 Industry has _____ .	1 Road traffic near the terminals has _____ .	1 _____ has been taken away from big ports. 2 Road traffic near the terminals has _____ .	1 There is a greater risk of _____ .

6.3 International trade – what are its effects?

Why trade?

Countries **trade** for a number of reasons:

- they cannot produce all they want or need;
- it is a way of making money;
- it is a way of gaining political influence.

International trade has a long history. An example is the European amber trade which began in the early Bronze Age, 5000 years ago. Amber is a fossilised resin with a golden-yellow colour which is valued as a gemstone (Fig 286). Deposits of amber are found only on the west coast of the Jutland Peninsula and on the south east shores of the Baltic Sea. However, amber jewellery dating from the early Bronze Age has been found in many European countries and the distribution of these finds is evidence for a series of land and sea trade routes (Fig 287).

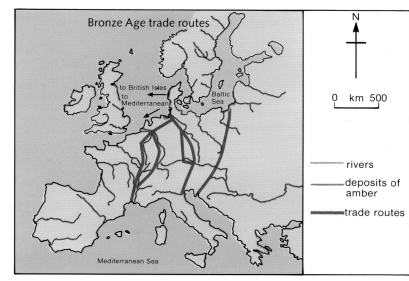

Fig 287 Bronze Age trade route

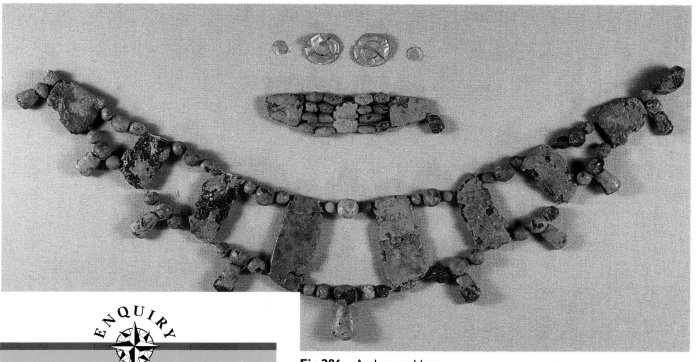

Fig 286 Amber necklace

ENQUIRY

Find out about the 'Silk Road'. Where was it? When and why was it important? Why did it become less important?

World trade links

In the nineteenth century a pattern of trade developed between Europe and its colonies. Europe imported (bought) raw materials (primary products) for its growing manufacturing industries, and food for its expanding towns and cities; and it exported (sold) manufactured goods (secondary products). The colonies exported raw materials and food, and imported manufactured goods.

To a large extent, this pattern still exists. MEDCs need raw materials which they get from LEDCs and MEDCs need manufactured goods which they get from MEDCs, a relationship described as interdependence.

However, the terms of trade – how much a country gets paid for its exports compared with how much it has to pay for its imports – are against the LEDCs because manufactured goods always cost more than raw materials. (This is because when you make something you have to pay for the factory, the machines, the labour force etc.) Consequently, LEDCs find themselves in a 'trade trap' because they always have to pay more for their imports than they earn from their exports.

In the 1980s the terms of trade for LEDCs got worse because of the world economic recesssion; over-production; and new materials such as synthetic fibres and plastics replacing traditional materials such as cotton and metal (Fig 288). Their exports earnt even less than they did before and as a result they became poorer and their debts increased (see Section 5.4).

Single product economies – countries which are dependent on the export of one or two raw materials – have suffered the most. For example, Sudan's main export is cotton but its price fell from 92 cents per pound in 1984 to 30 cents per pound in 1988.

It is difficult for LEDCs to break out of this 'trade trap' because they are at such a disadvantage. However, some have managed to do so (see Section 5.3 about East Asia's NICs) and overall they are slowly increasing their share of the world trade in manufactured goods (Fig 289).

Raw material:	cotton
Important to:	India, Sudan
Problem:	replaced by artificial fibres
Price:	1984 = 92 cents per pound
	1988 = 30 cents per pound

Raw material:	tin
Important to:	Columbia, Malaysia, Bolivia
Problem:	replaced by plastic
Price:	1984 = £8700 per tonne
	1988 = £4405 per tonne

Raw material:	cocoa
Important to:	Brazil, Colombia
Problem:	massive over-production
Price:	1984 = £2000 per tonne
	1988 = £800 per tonne

Fig 288   Changing terms of trade

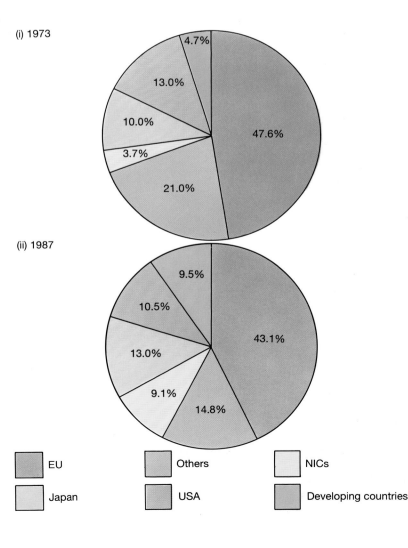

(i) 1973

(ii) 1987

EU   Others   NICs

Japan   USA   Developing countries

Fig 289   World trade in manufactured goods

ENQUIRY

1 Complete a copy of Fig 290 by deciding whether the main exports and imports of each country are raw materials or manufactured goods.
2 What do you notice about most of the exports and imports of **a)** the MEDCs and **b)** the LEDCs?
3 What exceptions are there to the general pattern and can you think of any possible explanations?

4 Add your own labels to a copy of Fig 291 to describe and explain the world pattern of trade.
5 Explain why the changing terms of trade have made the trade trap worse.
6 Describe the main changes shown in Fig 289.
7 What do you think would be the effect of the LEDCs putting up the cost of their raw materials?

Country	MEDC or LEDC	Exports	Raw materials or manufactured goods?	Imports	Raw materials or manufactured goods?
Australia		farm produce/ metal ores		machinery	
Bangladesh		jute		machinery	
Cuba		sugar		oil	
Denmark		meat/dairy products		machinery	
Ghana		cocoa		machinery	
Hong Kong		textiles		machinery	
Iran		oil		machinery	
Italy		machinery		machinery	
Jamaica		bauxite		oil	
Japan		machinery		oil	
Kenya		coffee		machinery	
Peru		copper		machinery	
Sri Lanka		tea		machinery	
UK		machinery		machinery	
USA		machinery		machinery	

Fig 290 Main exports and imports of selected countries

International trade and economic groups

In order to make trade easier and/or fairer, many countries have organised themselves into **economic groups** (Fig 292). Some, like The Organisation of Petroleum Exporting Countries (OPEC) are concerned with a single product. Others, like the EU, are concerned with a wide range of trade matters.

OPEC was formed in 1959 when the multinational oil companies cut their payments to the oil producing countries. By taking a united stand against the multinationals, OPEC was able to restore some of the price cuts. During the 1960s, MEDCs became more and more dependent on imported oil and this gave OPEC a much stronger hand in negotiations; for example, between October and December 1973 it was able to increase prices by 400 per cent. More recently, a greater supply of non-OPEC oil, e.g from the North Sea, has taken prices down but OPEC remains a powerful organisation and a good example of how LEDCs can get a fairer deal from international trade, if their product is in demand and if they can work together.

Before the formation of the EU, various trade barriers existed between the member countries. In some cases these took the form of tariffs (a tax on imports) while in others they took the form of quotas (a limit on imports). One of the aims of the EU was to remove those trade barriers and this was achieved in 1992 with the creation of the 'single European market'. The effect of joining the EU on the UK's trade pattern is shown in Fig 293.

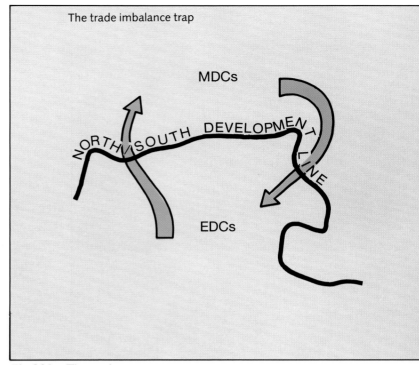

Fig 291   The trade trap

1   On an outline map of the world shade in and label the economic groups shown in Fig 292.
2   Why has OPEC been successful?
3   Describe and explain the effect of EU membership on the UK's trade pattern. What do you think are some of the consequences of these changes?
4   Read Fig 294. What are the advantages and disadvantages of the proposed North American Free Trade Agreement?

EU

ASEAN
(Association of South East Asian Nations)
Indonesia, Malaysia, Philippines,
Singapore, Thailand, Brunei

CACM
(Central American Common Market)
Costa Rica, Guatemala, El Salvador,
Honduras, Nicaragua

OPEC
(Organisation of Petroleum Exporting Countries)
Algeria, Ecuador, Gabon, Indonesia, Iran, Iraq,
Kuwait, Libya, Nigeria, Qatar, Saudi Arabia,
UAE, Venezuela

Fig 292   Some examples of economic groups

Multinationals and international trade

Multinationals (or transnationals) are large companies with operations in more than one country; for example, Pepsico, the world's biggest drinks company, has more than 500 factories and 335 000 workers in over 100 countries. The largest multinationals (Fig 295) have annual sales greater than the GNP of many LEDCs.

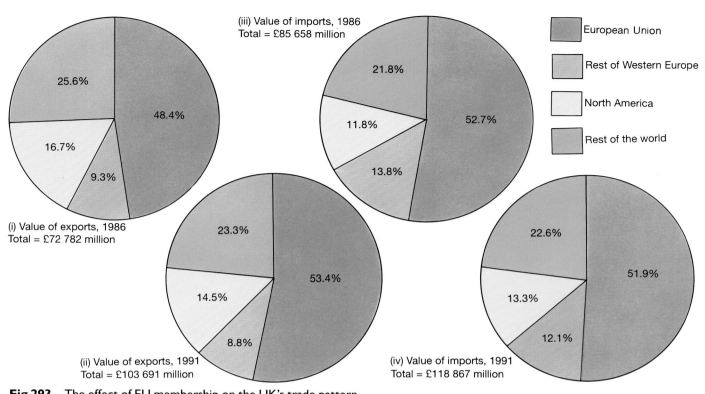

Fig 293 The effect of EU membership on the UK's trade pattern

(i) Value of exports, 1986
Total = £72 782 million

(ii) Value of exports, 1991
Total = £103 691 million

(iii) Value of imports, 1986
Total = £85 658 million

(iv) Value of imports, 1991
Total = £118 867 million

European Union

Rest of Western Europe

North America

Rest of the world

North America set for free trade zone

THE United States, Canada and Mexico reached final agreement yesterday on creating the world's largest free trade zone, embracing 370 million consumers and a combined gross national product of $6,400 billion (£4,387 billion).

In simultaneous announcements in Washington, Ottawa and Mexico City, the three countries declared their intention to implement the pact, known as the North American Free Trade Agreement (Nafta), by January 1 next year.

Yesterday's announcement will hasten the division of the world into ever more powerful economic and trading blocs. In terms of economic clout, the Nafta zone outstrips both the European Community and the Association of South-East Asian Nations. Like the EC, it has long-term potential for expansion – to include fast-developing South American economies such as Brazil.

But before it can be implemented, the agreement to abolish all tariff barriers must be ratified by congress in Mexico and the US. In Canada, additional legislation covering the supplemental pact is required.

In the US, there is strong opposition among labour unions and manufacturing interests, which fear jobs and profits will be lost to low-cost, low-wage Mexican competition.

Mexican officials yesterday sought to pre-empt criticism that they had caved in to US pressure in agreeing to potential trade sanctions. "The out-come will allow Mexico . . . to improve the living standards of its people and to protect its environment," the trade minister, Jaime Serra, said.

The Guardian, 14 August 1993

Fig 294 The North American Free Trade Agreement

Company	Industry	Headquarters	Sales (US $ billions)
General Motors	Vehicles	USA	123.7
Royal Dutch/Shell	Oil refining	UK/Netherlands	103.8
IBM	Computers	USA	65.3
General Electric	Electronics	USA	60.2
Philip Morris	Food	USA	48.1
El du Pont	Chemicals	USA	38.0
Boeing	Aerospace	USA	29.3
Asea Brown Boveri	Industrial/farm equipment	Switzerland	28.8
Procter and Gamble	Soaps/cosmetics	USA	27.4
Pepsico	Drinks	USA	19.7

The New Internationalist, August 1993

Fig 295   The world's ten largest multinationals 1991

There are a total of 35 000 multinationals and they control 70 per cent of world trade. More than 90 per cent of these companies are based in MEDCs and this reinforces the 'trade trap', because although they have operations in LEDCs they take away most of the profit; for example, between 1965-6 and 1975-6 multinationals in India sent back £333 million of profit to their parent companies.

Fig 296 shows that multinational investment in LEDCs is increasing. This is because of a number of factors including lower wage rates, less strict planning regulations and requirements laid down by the IMF and the World Bank to LEDCs seeking help.

Governments in LEDCs find themselves in a difficult position where multinationals are concerned. Although they take away most of the profit, they do not take all of it; and they also bring jobs and advanced technology.

Some countries have tried to limit the number of multinationals, or to control their operations more closely. However, such policies have had limited success. In fact, in 1991, 30 LEDCs made it easier for multinationals to invest, not harder.

For example, rather than get rid of multinationals completely, the Indian Government in the 1970s and 1980s tried to reduce the foreign share-holding and increase the Indian share-holding in order to keep more of the profit in the country. This policy was known as 'Indianisation' but its main effect was to put multinationals off completely. In the 1990s it decided to follow a new policy of encouraging the multinationals and in the period 1990-3 it agreed proposals for foreign investments of £500 million; Pepsico, Sony, Kellogg's and other 'world brands' are now operating in the country for the first time.

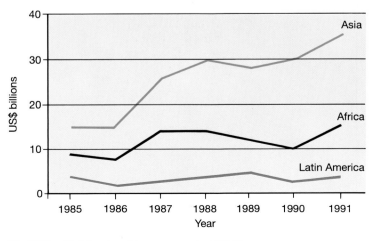

Fig 296   Multinational investment in LEDCs

1 On an outline map of the world, mark on and label the ten largest multinationals and their headquarters. Describe and comment on their distribution.
2 Why do multinationals make the trade trap worse?
3 Imagine that you work for the Ministry of Economic Development in a LEDC. A multinational has asked for permission to buy farmland and to build a food processing plant. Their aim is to grow fruit for drinks and canning. Write a report for your Minister explaining clearly the advantages and disadvantages of the proposal, both for your country and for the multinational. At the end of your report state whether or not you think permission should be granted, and explain why.

What is the future for international trade?

In the 1930s many countries put up trade barriers to protect their own industries because of the world recession. This brought trade to a virtual stand still and it had disastrous economic consequences. In 1948, in order to stop this from happening again, 23 of the world's richest countries signed the General Agreement on Tariffs and Trade (GATT).

GATT has become the world's most important trade negotiating body, although its members do not always agree with each other. In 1986 a round of negotiations began in Uruguay and continued until December 1993: however, with an estimated increase in world economic output of more than five trillion dollars at stake, this is perhaps understandable!

GATT has achieved its main aim of stabilising world trade. However, it has done little to help LEDCs because it has encouraged them to concentrate on exporting raw materials; consequently it has reinforced the trade trap.

Other international agreements have also reinforced the existing pattern of trade. For example, the Lomé Convention is an agreement between the EC and over 60 LEDCs; in one sense it helps these countries because it gives them tariff-free entry to the EC for their raw materials and foodstuffs but it does little to stimulate their manufacturing industries.

However, there have been changes which have allowed at least some LEDCs to benefit more from the world trade system. Overall, manufacturing exports from LEDCs have risen (see Fig 289, page 178) and the list of NICs has grown. For example, Malaysia exported its first 10 000 Proton cars to Europe in 1989 (Fig 297).

A number of reasons help to explain these changes. The Governments of many of these countries have invested a great deal of money in training workers, developing infrastructure (roads, electricity, water etc) and setting up industries. Transport costs have gone down because ships are bigger and modern materials weigh less. Also, groups like the United Nations Conference on Trade and Development (UNCTAD) have had some success in making international agreements fairer for LEDCs.

Operating at a smaller, but not insignificant scale, are Alternative Trading Organisations (**ATOs**). These are companies based in MEDCs which import handmade products and foodstuffs from LEDCs at a fairer price. They usually sell through mail order catalogues and although prices are generally more expensive than those found in the High Street shops they are of guaranteed quality and a 'little bit different'.

Traidcraft is the second largest ATO in the UK, after Oxfam. One group it is involved with is a co-operative in Mujurpet in southern India which is run by the women of the village. They make items such as baskets out of palm leaves, and Traidcraft helps them with the design of new products and the red tape which surrounds international trade. It takes a day to make a basket and for this the women earn 60p. This may not sound a lot but it is twice the amount they would earn as farm labourers.

The women have benefited from the co-operative in many ways: their income has increased; they have the chance to save; they have learned skills; they have had the opportunity to travel; they have achieved greater independence; and they have found themselves with a new voice in village affairs.

Buying a new car? Proton guarantee you the best quotes

What's made the twelve-strong Proton range of saloons and hatchbacks win the acclaim of the British Motoring Press?

Proton quality. Reliability. And outstanding value for money.

It's down to responsive Japanese derived Triple-Valve engines with Multi-Point fuel injection and 3-way catalytic converters. Backed by a 6 Year/60,000 miles Power-Train Warranty.

It's also down to a 6 Year Bodywork Warranty++ (thanks to Galvannealed Steel key body panels) and a 2 Year/50,000 miles Total Vehicle Warranty.

And it's down to specification, with cars available with central locking, electric windows, tilt/slide sunroofs and Blaupunkt digital stereo radin/cassette systems.

Many are fitted with power steering. Others come

JAPANESE ◆ TECHNOLOGY
Malaysian Value

For further details of Proton cars and our special purchase plans, visit your Proton dealer.
You can be sure of the best quotes.

OVER 230 DEALERS NATIONWIDE

£6,990 - £9,490
(Excluding delivery and number plates).

with automatic transmission. Even air conditioning is available. And they all come with 2 Years Free RAC Membership and the Proton Security System, making your car over 150 times less likely to be stolen.

Proton cars hold their value longer too, thanks to residual values that are amongst the highest of any marque. Plus, if you're a company car driver, Proton's are even better value. With income tax liability soon to be charged on the basis of manufacturer's list prices, business users will make substantial tax savings compared with other similarly specified but more highly priced marques. No wonder 99% of customers are 100% satisfied and to prove it, well over 50,000 Proton cars have been sold in the UK in just four years.

Fig 297   Proton advertisement

In 1970 there were only a few ATOs worldwide, with less than £500 000 sales between them. However, by 1987 there were more than 50, with a combined annual sales figure of more than £35 million. They have set up the International Federation for Alternative Trade (IFAT) to coordinate their activities.

ENQUIRY

1 What have been the advantages and disadvantages of GATT, and to whom?

2 Why does increasing their manufactured exports help LEDCs to get a fairer deal from world trade?

3 Why do you think Japan, rather than Malaysia (where the car is made), gets most mention in the advertisement, Fig 297?

4 In what ways, other than economic, has the Mujurpet co-operative benefited from fairer trade?

5 Although not insignificant, why is the overall impact of ATOs likely to be limited?

6 What does Fig 298 tell us about the world trade system?

Fig 298 An extract from the Traidcraft Exchange Magazine

6.4 Assessment Task: *A fairer deal*

Imagine that you are the Minister of Trade for Ghana. Some important economic indicators and statistics are given about your country in Fig 299. However, before you represent Ghana in the latest round of GATT negotiations, you had better find out some more! Find Ghana in an atlas: make notes, and draw at least one sketch map to describe its location, relief, climate, land use and raw materials.

The GATT negotiations are at a difficult stage. The USA is threatening to put tariffs on a range of food imports because it thinks its own farmers are being treated unfairly. (Some countries are protecting their farmers by giving them subsidies so that they can sell their produce at a lower price than imported food from the USA.)

One of the crops the USA is threatening to put a tariff on is cocoa, which is Ghana's main export. If the move goes ahead, it will present your country with real problems.

Write a speech which includes the following:

- A description of your country's pattern of trade, and an analysis of the problems it causes.
- An explanation of why trade became more of a problem for Ghana during the 1980s.
- An account of how and why tariffs would affect Ghana.
- A prediction of the likely consequences on trade patterns in general, if the USA goes ahead with its threat.

Fig 299 Ghana: vital statistics

Ghana: a fact file

Area	238 540 km^2	Food supply	2144 calories per person per day
Population	16.7 million	Main exports	cocoa, gold, timber
Population increase	3.5% per year	Main destination of exports	Switzerland, UK, Russia
GNP	400 US$ per person per year	Main imports	oil, machinery, chemicals
Source of GNP		Main source of imports	Nigeria, UK, Germany
a) agriculture 53%		Trade deficit	251 million US$ (1992)
b) manufacturing 17%			
c) services 30%			

GLOSSARY

accessibility   how easy a place is to get to.

age structure   the percentage of people in different age groups and in a population.

agglomeration   a group of industries in the same location.

agribusiness   large-scale **commercial farming** run by agricultural companies.

ATOs   Alternative Trading Organisations: companies which **trade** with LEDCs but on a fairer basis than is usual.

appropriate technology   equipment etc, which is suitable for the country in which it is being used; it usually refers to simple, low cost ways of doing things.

arable farm   one which specialises in producing crops.

area payments subsidies   given to farmers according to how many acres of a crop they grow.

backwash effect   the process by which a **core** region attracts people, materials and money from a **peripheral** region.

beef premium   a subsidy given to farmers according to how many cattle they keep, and for how long.

bilateral aid   money or help given by one Government to another.

birth rate   the number of babies born per 1000 people per year.

break of bulk point   the place where goods have to be unloaded e.g. a port.

capital intensive   an activity which requires a lot of money.

census   a counting of people.

CBD   Central Business District: the zone of shops and offices in a town or city centre.

central place   a settlement which provides goods and services for the places around it.

colonies   countries run by another country.

commercial farm   one which produces crops etc mainly for sale.

CAP   Common Agricultural Policy: the policy used by the European Community to control farming.

commuter   a person who travels to work, particularly from the suburbs or a smaller settlement to the business district of a town or city.

comparison goods/services   things we shop around for to compare prices e.g. clothes.

comprehensive redevelopment   a planning strategy which involves demolishing run down buildings and replacing them with new ones.

containerisation   goods being packed into large metal boxes for transport by road and/or sea.

contraception   using birth control to stop pregnancy.

conurbation   a large urban settlement which is the result of towns and cities spreading out and merging together.

convenience goods/services   things we need to buy regularly e.g. bread.

co-operatives   groups of workers who join together to share things e.g. farmers sharing a milk processing plant, or machinery.

core region   an area at the heart of economic activity e.g. a well-off industrial region of a country.

cumulative causation   the process by which one region of a country becomes increasingly the centre of economic activity.

death rate   the number of deaths per 1000 people per year.

delta   a low-lying area of land deposited at the mouth of a river.

demographic transition   the change from high **birth** and **death rates** to low birth and death rates.

dependant population   those who rely on the **working population** for support e.g. the young and the elderly.

dependency   the unequal relationship between a **metropole** and a **satellite**.

de-urbanisation   the process by which an increasingly smaller percentage of a country's population lives in towns and cities, brought about by urban-rural migration.

development line   an imaginary line separating MEDCs from LEDCs.

dormitory settlement   one where many **commuters** 'sleep' in it but travel to work elsewhere.

economic group   countries which have joined together to make trade etc, easier.

economic recession   a time when the economy gets worse and people lose their jobs

ethnic race   the group of people a person belongs to.

extensive farm   one with low **inputs**: they usually cover a large area and have a low **output** per acre.

factory farming   keeping animals in artificial conditions indoors.

family planning   using **contraception** to control the size of your family.

fixed industry   one which is tied to a particular location.

footloose industry   one which could set up in many different locations.

foreign aid   help given to another country.

formal sector   a 'proper job' e.g. in a factory.

free range   allowing animals to move about a sizeable area.

GATT   General Agreement on Tariffs and Trade: an agreement to control international trade.

gentrification   this is when an area of a town or city is renovated and then occupied by better off people.

green belt a ring of land surrounding a town or city upon which no new building is allowed.

green revolution a high-technology approach to increasing agricultural production: it is particularly associated with **HYVs**.

GDP Gross Domestic Product: this is a similar statistic to GNP i.e. it is how much a county earns but it does not include income from foreign investments etc.

GNP Gross National Produicts is the amount a country earns in a year.

guaranteed prices a type of farm subsidy: the farmer is guaranteed a minimum price for everything produced.

guest-worker migration people leaving their country to work in another land but not to settle: the term is associated with unskilled/semi-skilled labour.

heavy industry one with heavy/bulky raw materials and heavy/bulky finished products.

hierarchy a rank order e.g. of settlements according to size of population.

high-technology industry one which makes computers, electronic components, etc.

HYVs High Yielding Varieties: new types of seed which have been scientifically developed to produce more food per plant.

hinterland the area served by a port.

huertas irrigated farms in Spain.

industrial revolution the growth and development of manufacturing industry and the factory system which began in the UK in the eighteenth century.

infant mortality the number of babies dying before their first birthday per 1000 births.

informal sector casual, irregular work e.g. street-selling.

inner city the zone surrounding the **Central Business Distict** of a town or city: it is often very run down.

inputs the things needed to run a factory or farm e.g. raw materials, fertiliser.

integrated iron and steel works a large factory in which all stages of iron and steel production are carried out.

integration different groups of people living and working together.

intensive farm one with high inputs and outputs.

international debt the money owed by LEDCs to MEDCs.

irrigation adding water to land to make it productive.

large-scale aid help which involves large amounts of money and/or assistance.

latifundia large farming estates in Spain.

LEDCs the poorer, Less Economically Developed Countries of mainly South America, Africa and Asia.

light industry manufacturing industry which has light raw materials and finished products.

linear settlement a settlement which follows the line of, for example, a road or river.

long-term aid help which continues for a number of years.

loose-knit settlement a settlement with many gaps between its buildings and little, if any, pattern.

Manufacturing Belt the region of traditional, often **heavy industry** in the north of the USA.

market gardens farms which produce vegetables, fruit and flowers.

MEDCs the richer, More Economically Developed Countries of mainly North Amerrica, Europe and Australasia.

megalopolis a continuous stretch of urban settlement which results from towns, cities and **conurbations** merging together.

metropoles rich, industrialised countries which dominate **satellites**.

migration people moving from one place to live in another.

military aid weapons given to people fighting a war

minifundia small-scale subsistence farms in Spain.

million city a city with more than a million inhabitants.

mixed farm one which produces crops and animals.

multilateral aid money or help given by a Government or an international organisation which then decides how to use it.

multinational a large company with operations in more than one country.

multiplier effect the 'snowballing' of economic activity e.g. if new jobs are created in a city, the people who take them have money to spend in the shops, which means that more shop workers are needed etc.

natural increase the rate at which a country's population is going up because of the difference between the birth rate and the death rate.

New Towns towns designed from scratch as a fresh start for urban living.

NICs Newly Industrialising Countries: LEDCs which are developing manufacturing industry.

nomadic herding a way of farming which involves moving with your animals to new grazing and/or water holes.

nucleated settlement a settlement which is clustered around a particular point.

occupational structure the balance between the different sectors of the economy e.g. **primary, secondary, tertiary, quarternary**.

outputs the end products, e.g. what a factory makes, what a farm grows

overspill estates estates built to rehouse people from run down areas of the **inner city**.

pastoral farm one which specialises in the production of animals/animal products.

pedestrianisation making areas of towns and cities accessible for people on foot only.

peripheral region an area on the fringe of economic activity e.g. a poor, backward region of a country.

plantation a large farm in the tropics which specialises in the production of a single crop.

population density the number of people in a given area.

population distribution   the spread of people throughout a region or country.

population pyramid   a graph which shows the **age and sex structure** of a place.

primary industry   one which gets raw materials from the ground, the sea or the air.

processes   the activities which take place in a factory or on a farm e.g. rolling out steel, or harvesting.

pull factors   the things which attract someone to migrate to a place.

push factors   the things which force someone out of a place.

quarternary industry   one which uses modern technology to carry out research, handle information and give advice.

quota   a limit to the amount which can be produced/sold/traded etc.

racial prejudice   thinking things about people because of the colour of their skin and/or their ethnic group without knowing them.

range of good   how far someone is prepared to travel for a particular good or service.

repatriation   returning immigrants to their country of origin.

residential preference   where people would like to live.

roll-on/roll-off   ferries which are designed to allow lorries to drive on and off without having to unload their **containers**.

rural-urban migration   the movement of people from the countryside to the town.

satellites   LEDCs dominated by **metropoles**.

secondary industry   one which makes finished products out of raw materials i.e. manufacturing industry.

segregation   different groups of people living and working apart.

set aside   a scheme set up by the **CAP** which requires arable farmers not to grow crops on 15 per cent of their land in return for area payments on their other crops.

settlement   a place where people live

shifting cultivation   a traditional system of farming in the tropics which involves moving to a new area of land every few years when the existing fields lose their fertility.

short-term aid   help given for a small amount of time

single product economy   a country which relies on one, or a very small number, of products for its export earnings.

site   the land upon which, for example, a settlement or factory is built.

situation   a settlement or factory, for example, in relation to the area around it: roads, rivers, land use etc.

small-scale aid   help that involves very little money and/or equipment.

social leap-frogging   the process by which those who can afford to do so move out of an area as it becomes older and more run down, to be replaced by less well-off people.

sphere of influence   the area a settlement serves.

spread effect   people, materials and money moving from a **core region** to a **peripheral region**.

squatter settlement   an area of makeshift housing lived in by (mainly) rural-urban migrants: most cities in LEDCs have them and they are given various local names e.g. bustees (Calcutta), favelas (Brazil).

sterilisation   a method of **contraception**: in men an operation prevents sperm from being released, and in women an operation stops the production of eggs.

subsidies   payments given e.g. to farmers to make up their income.

subsistence farm   one producing food mainly for the family to eat.

suburbanisation   the growth of suburbs – residential zones – in towns and cities.

Sunbelt   a growth region of often **high-technology industry** in the south of the USA.

tertiary industry   one which produces a service.

thematic maps   ones which give information about a particular feature of a country or region e.g. its climate or its farming.

threshold of entry   the size a settlement has to be before it can offer a particular good or service.

trade   the exchange of goods and/or services.

transhipment   this is when a large cargo is unloaded and put into smaller ships to be taken to its final destination.

urban renewal   a planning strategy which involves renovating buildings rather than knocking them down.

urbanisation   the process by which an increasing percentage of a country's population comes to live in towns and cities.

voluntary aid   money and/or help given by charities.

working population   people in employment who have to support the dependent population.

INDEX